HELSINKI TRAVEL GUIDE

The Ultimate Book To Uncovering Helsinki's Hidden Gem

Patrick Wilson

Copyright © by **Patrick Wilson**

All rights reserved. No part of this book may be reproduced in any form or by any means, including photocopying, recording, or by any information storage and retrieval system, without permission in writing from the publisher, except for brief quotations in reviews or articles.

Disclaimer: The views and opinions expressed in this book are those of the author and do not necessarily reflect the official policy or position or any other organization.

Table of Contents

Brief History 6
Geography 9
Tourists Must Know Things Before Visiting 12
Best Touring Apps and websites 15
Top Activities 18
    Hiking 18
    Swimming 21
    Cruises and Boating 24
    Canoeing & Kayaking 27
    Golf 30
    Ice Skating 33
    Cross-country Skiing 35
Dialects and Language 38
Weather 41
Getting Here 44
Top Attractions 47
    Suomenlinna Fortress 47
    Helsinki Cathedral 50
    Uspenski Cathedral 53
    Temppeliaukio Church (Rock Church) 56
    Seurasaari Open-Air Museum 59
    Sibelius Monument 62

Ateneum Art Museum 65
National Museum of Finland 68
Kiasma Museum of Contemporary Art 71
Esplanade Park 73
Design Museum Helsinki 75
Helsinki Zoo 78
Linnanmäki Amusement Park 81
Museum of Finnish Architecture 84
Havis Amanda Statue 86
Parliament House 89
Helsinki Olympic Stadium 92
Kamppi Chapel of Silence 95
Museum of Natural History 98
Suomen Kansallisooppera (Finnish National Opera) 101
Kallio District 103

Top Cuisine to Try Out 106
Kalakukko 106
Karjalanpiirakka 108
Lohikeitto 110
Hernekeitto 112
Poronkäristys 114
Silakkapihvit 116

Ruisleipä 118
Salmiakki 120
Mustikkapiirakka 122
Korvapuusti 124
Best Time To Visit 127
Traveling Itinerary 130
Visiting On a Budget 133
Getting Around 136
Shopping for Souvenirs 139
Tour Package Options 142
Tourist Safety Tips 145
Festival and Events 148

Brief History

Helsinki, the dynamic capital of Finland, possesses a rich and interesting history that spans centuries, including influences from numerous cultures and eras. From its humble beginnings as a small fishing hamlet to its current status as a modern European city, Helsinki's evolution is a riveting tale of expansion, resilience, and cultural fusion.

The foundations of Helsinki's history may be traced back to the 16th century when the area was part of the Swedish Kingdom. In 1550, King Gustav Vasa of Sweden created the city of Helsinki to challenge the successful commercial metropolis of Tallinn in nearby Estonia. The city was ideally positioned on the southern shore, allowing access to the Baltic Sea and aiding trade routes. Over the next two decades, Helsinki's role as a trade port rose, bringing merchants and settlers.

In 1809, Finland was transferred to Russia as an autonomous Grand Duchy, and Helsinki became the capital of the newly constituted autonomous Finnish region. The Russian influence is obvious in the city's architecture, with several neoclassical structures completed during this period. One of the most recognizable structures, the Helsinki Cathedral, was finished in 1852 and stands as a reminder of the city's ties to the Russian past.

The late 19th century brought an awakening of Finnish national identity and a drive for greater autonomy. The Finnish language, arts, and culture gained popularity, and Helsinki became a center for Finnish literature and intellectual thought. The Ateneum Art Museum, founded in 1887, symbolizes this era's cultural significance, housing an extensive collection of Finnish art from this period.

The early 20th century was marked by substantial political changes. Finland declared independence from Russia in 1917, and Helsinki became the capital of the newly constituted republic. The coming years were hard, with civil conflict and global turmoil defining the nation's trajectory. The Winter War (1939-1940) and the Continuation War (1941-1944) against the Soviet Union left enduring wounds on the city, although Helsinki emerged from these conflicts with its spirit intact.

The post-war years brought forth a time of significant urbanization and modernization. Helsinki hosted the 1952 Summer Olympics, exhibiting its fresh energy to the globe. The city's architecture changed again, adopting functionalist forms and innovative urban planning. The Sibelius Monument, dedicated to the famed Finnish musician, Jean Sibelius, is a significant example of modernist sculpture that serves as a tribute to this era.

By the late 20th century, Helsinki had established itself as a magnet of innovation and creativity. The foundation of the University of Helsinki in 1829 provided the groundwork for the city's position as a hub of education and research. The rise of design and technology businesses further established Helsinki's modern identity. The renowned Design District and the establishment of corporations like Nokia played crucial roles in establishing the city's present image.

Today, Helsinki stands as a lively metropolis noted for its modern architecture, progressive urban planning, and great quality of life. The city's historical landmarks combine perfectly with sleek, contemporary designs, creating a unique visual landscape. Tourists are lured to sights like the historic Suomenlinna Sea Fortress, a UNESCO World Heritage site, which depicts centuries of Finnish military history.

Conclusion

Helsinki's history is a captivating trip that depicts its rise from a humble trading port to a booming European powerhouse. The city's unique blend of architectural influences, cultural achievements, and historical events provides tourists with a fascinating tapestry to explore. From its Swedish and Russian roots to its rise as a powerhouse of innovation, Helsinki's history is a monument to the endurance and flexibility of its people.

Geography

Helsinki is a dynamic and culturally rich metropolis located on the southern coast of the country. Its topographical factors have played a vital effect in creating the city's development and identity. From its strategic position along the Gulf of Finland to its unique urban layout, Helsinki's geography has played a crucial role in its historical, economic, and social history.

Situated on the southern tip of the peninsula that extends into the Gulf of Finland, Helsinki benefits from a coastline location that has historically enabled trade and maritime links. The city's harbor has been a vital gateway for commodities and people, contributing to its emergence as a major regional center. The presence of the sea has also influenced the city's climate, resulting in somewhat milder temperatures compared to other places in Finland. This maritime impact plays a role in making Helsinki an appealing place for both tourists and businesses.

The archipelago around Helsinki is another geographical factor that contributes to its peculiar character. With various islands dotting the neighboring waters, the city features a unique blend of urban and natural environments. Many of these islands are accessible by ferries and have become recreational destinations for locals and visitors alike. The interaction between the city and the archipelago illustrates the intertwining of urban development and nature, adding to Helsinki's attraction as a destination that offers both modern conveniences and natural beauty.

Helsinki's urban planning and layout indicate a careful commitment to utilizing its geography. The city's center section is arranged on a north-south axis, with major streets running along the shoreline. This design not only increases access to the coastline but also enhances navigability within the city. The presence of parks, natural areas, and tree-lined avenues further highlights the city's commitment to combining urban living with nature. This strategy has resulted in Helsinki being recognized for its great quality of life and sustainable urban development.

The location of Helsinki has also influenced its economic activities. The city's location along important trade routes has historically made it a center for commerce and transportation. The well-connected harbor facilities have aided the transit of products, and Helsinki's closeness to other Baltic Sea countries has promoted commercial partnerships. Additionally, the city's airport, situated a short distance from the downtown, has contributed to its role as a regional gateway for international travel.

Helsinki's geographical situation has not only molded its physical landscape but has also contributed to its cultural identity. The city's historical contacts with surrounding countries, especially Sweden and Russia, have resulted in a blend of architectural styles and cultural influences. This eclectic background is represented in the city's buildings, museums, and cultural organizations. Helsinki's topography has also played a role in the development of its renowned design and architectural scene, with the surrounding landscape often providing a source of inspiration for local creatives.

Conclusion

The topography of Helsinki is a diverse component that has greatly impacted the city's development, identity, and way of life. Its coastal position, archipelago, urban design, and economic prospects have all played a role in molding the city into a contemporary, forward-thinking metropolis that mixes urban living with nature. Helsinki's interaction with its surroundings and its strategic position in the Baltic area continue to impact its trajectory as a global city with a distinct and appealing geographical character.

Tourists Must Know Things Before Visiting

Before going on your journey to this wonderful city of Helsinki, let's look into some crucial information that every visitor should know to make the most of their visit.

Currency and Payment
The Country's official currency used in Helsinki is the Euro (EUR). Credit and debit cards are generally accepted throughout the city, so you won't need to carry huge quantities of cash. However, it's a good idea to have extra cash on hand for smaller sellers and establishments that might not accept cards.

Cultural Etiquette
Finns are recognized for their politeness and restrained temperament. It's usual to greet someone with a handshake and make close eye contact. Tipping isn't a big element of Finnish society, but it's growing more frequent in tourist-heavy locations. Always check if a service charge is included in your bill before leaving an additional tip.

Sauna Culture
Saunas are an intrinsic element of Finnish culture, and no visit to Helsinki is complete without visiting a typical Finnish sauna. Whether in public saunas or private accommodations, it's an opportunity to relax, unwind, and embrace a local habit. Remember to follow sauna etiquette by showering before entering and carrying a towel to sit on.

Dining and Cuisine

Helsinki's culinary culture offers a delicious blend of traditional Finnish foods and international influences. Don't miss the chance to enjoy local specialties such as reindeer meals, fish, and Karelian pastries. Explore the Market Square for a sample of street cuisine, then venture to the many restaurants and cafes for a diversified gastronomic experience.

Safety and Health

Helsinki is generally regarded as a safe place for travelers. However, it's recommended to take normal precautions, such as preserving your things and being mindful of your surroundings. The city's tap water is safe to drink, so there's no need to rely on bottled water.

Accommodation Options

When it comes to locating a place to stay, Helsinki offers a selection of housing alternatives to meet different budgets and preferences. From opulent hotels with beautiful waterfront views to charming boutique guesthouses and budget-friendly hostels, there's something for everyone. Consider lodging near the city center to have easy access to main attractions and transportation hubs.

Public Saunas and Sea Swimming

Public saunas like Löyly and Allas Sea Pool put a modern touch on this ancient habit, allowing you to relax in a warm and tranquil environment. If you're feeling daring, take a cool dip in the Baltic Sea following your sauna session—a habit that's popular among locals year-round.

Environmental Consciousness

Finland places a great focus on sustainability and environmental sensitivity. You'll find recycling bins throughout the city, and it's expected that you'll engage in appropriate garbage disposal. Consider limiting your plastic usage and opting for reusable things that match local values.

Time for Relaxation
While experiencing Helsinki's lively culture and attractions is a must, don't forget to leave aside time for leisure. Take leisurely walks around the waterfront, enjoy a cup of coffee at a neighborhood cafe, or simply absorb the serene atmosphere that Helsinki offers.

Emergency Numbers
In case of any emergencies, phone 112 for police, medical help, or fire services. It's always a good idea to have these numbers ready in case you need assistance during your stay.

Conclusion
Helsinki is a city that smoothly integrates modernity with heritage, offering a vast selection of experiences for every style of traveler. By being prepared with these insights, you'll have the information needed to fully enjoy all that Helsinki has to offer. Whether you're visiting its ancient buildings, delighting in gastronomic delicacies, or immersing yourself in its sauna culture, your visit to Helsinki is guaranteed to be a memorable and enriching adventure.

Best Touring Apps and websites

Exploring a bustling city like Helsinki has never been easier, due to a number of touring apps and websites that give thorough information and easy tools for travelers. Whether you're seeking historical sites, local food, or hidden jewels, these internet platforms may dramatically enhance your vacation experience

TripAdvisor
TripAdvisor offers user-generated reviews and ratings for hotels, restaurants, and attractions in Helsinki. It's a helpful resource for judging the quality and popularity of various possibilities. You may also book hotels and restaurants straight through the platform.
Website: *www.tripadvisor.com/Tourism-g189934-Helsinki_Uusimaa-Hotels.html*

Google Maps
Google Maps is a vital tool for navigating any city. In Helsinki, it provides real-time instructions for walking, driving, and public transportation. You may browse neighboring attractions, examine street-level photos, and read user reviews. The "Explore" section indicates popular places to visit and dine.
Website: *www.google.com/maps*

Like A Local Guide
For those seeking an authentic local experience, Like A Local Guide delivers insights from residents. Discover off-the-beaten-path sites, restaurants, and activities that may not be mentioned in a conventional guidebook.
Website: *www.likealocalguide.com/helsinki*

Helsinki Design District
Helsinki is famed for its design legacy. The Helsinki Design District website provides information about design-focused stores, galleries, and studios.
Website: *www.designdistrict.fi/*

Helsinki Card
The Helsinki Card offers a complete method to experience the city's greatest attractions and public transportation. It allows free access to several museums and sights, as well as savings on excursions and restaurants. The companion app lets you schedule your visits and keep track of your savings.
Website: *www.helsinkicard.com/*

MyHelsinki.fi
MyHelsinki.fi is the official tourism website for Helsinki. It offers a variety of information about activities, events, food, shopping, and lodgings. The site's "Local Tips" section contains advice from Helsinki residents themselves.
Website: *www.myhelsinki.fi/en*

Culture Trip
Culture Trip provides handpicked articles and recommendations on various elements of Helsinki, including art, food, history, and more. It gives in-depth insights into the city's culture and lifestyle, making it a terrific resource for those interested in a deeper understanding of Helsinki.
Website: *www.theculturetrip.com/europe/finland/helsinki/*

Rent a Finn
For a unique and immersive experience, try using the "Rent a Finn" program. This campaign allows visitors to meet with

locals and experience true Finnish friendliness. Through the website, you may schedule experiences with Finns who share their way of life and introduce you to Finnish nature and culture.
Website: *www.visitfinland.com/en/*

GetYourGuide
GetYourGuide offers a wide choice of tours and activities in Helsinki, allowing you to book experiences directly through the platform. Whether you're interested in guided city tours, boat cruises, or outdoor excursions, this website provides many options to pick from.
Website: *www.getyourguide.com/helsinki-l13/*

Instagram
Social media outlets like Instagram can also be useful sources of inspiration for your Helsinki vacation. Follow hashtags like #VisitHelsinki or #HelsinkiTravel to uncover gorgeous photographs of the city's landmarks, architecture, and local culture.

Conclusion
Helsinki's touring apps and websites offer a varied selection of possibilities to enhance your trip experience. From official city guides to user-generated reviews, local insights, and unique experiences, these digital resources cater to every style of tourist. Whether you're interested in history, design, gastronomy, or nature, there's a platform that can help you make the most of your stay in Helsinki.

Top Activities

Helsinki stands as a vibrant and scenic destination that offers a wealth of outdoor activities for the avid traveler, with its stunning landscapes, tranquil water bodies, and well-maintained parks, this Nordic treasure calls to those who seek adventure and rejuvenation in the lap of nature. From exciting treks to calm waterfront excursions, Helsinki's physical outdoor activities offer a varied range of preferences and interests. Here are some outdoor activities you can enjoy as a tourist in Helsinki:

Hiking

Nestled just a short drive away from Helsinki, Nuuksio National Park offers a mesmerizing getaway into Finland's natural environment. With its lush forests, tranquil lakes, and rich flora and fauna, Nuuksio is an excellent location for trekking enthusiasts and nature lovers alike.

Located around 30 kilometers from Helsinki, Nuuksio National Park is easily accessible by vehicle or public transportation. Travelers seeking an immersive experience can jump on a bus or take a train to the park's surroundings and then follow clearly indicated trails to the main gate. To guarantee a seamless journey, consider checking the park's official website for up-to-date information on transit choices, operating hours, and any entry fees.

Nuuksio National Park provides a network of well-maintained trails suited to hikers of varying skill levels. From easy strolls to demanding climbs, the park offers something for everyone. Beginners might opt for shorter paths like the Korpinkierros loop, while more experienced hikers could love the difficult terrain of the Haukankierros trail. Each trail provides an opportunity to experience diverse parts of the park's natural splendor, including ancient forests, steep hills, and stunning lakes.

The park's diversified ecosystem shows an assortment of plant and animal species unique to the Finnish wilderness. As you trek through the paths, keep a look out for brilliant wildflowers, towering pine trees, and delicate moss carpets. Lucky visitors might even glimpse elusive wildlife such as deer, foxes, and other bird species. Nuuksio's calm and pristine surroundings make it a perfect destination for nature photographers and wildlife aficionados.

One of the beauties of Nuuksio National Park is its numerous crystal-clear lakes and ponds. Many hiking routes make their way down the shoreline, allowing opportunities for tranquil picnics, fishing, or simply enjoying the calming sights. The calm environment of these aquatic bodies is great for unwinding and connecting with nature.

For those seeking to extend their stay, Nuuksio offers designated camping spots where visitors can pitch tents and immerse themselves in the park's ambiance. Additionally, various neighboring hotels, including lodges and cabins, give a nice getaway after a day of exploration. Early reservations are recommended, especially during peak tourist seasons.

Nuuksio National Park endures fascinating transformations throughout the year, each season giving a distinct experience. Spring and summer bring lush greenery and blooming flowers, making it a perfect season for birdwatching and capturing beautiful landscapes. Fall covers the park in warm colors, luring photographers and hikers seeking magnificent autumn panoramas. In winter, the pathways transform into a snowy wonderland, inviting cross-country skiers and snowshoeing lovers to experience the park's quiet beauty in a new light.

Preserving Nuuksio's pure ecosystem is of vital importance. As you explore the trails, remember to adhere to the principles of "Leave No Trace." This involves packing out any rubbish, staying on authorized trails, and protecting the natural habitats of plants and animals.

Swimming

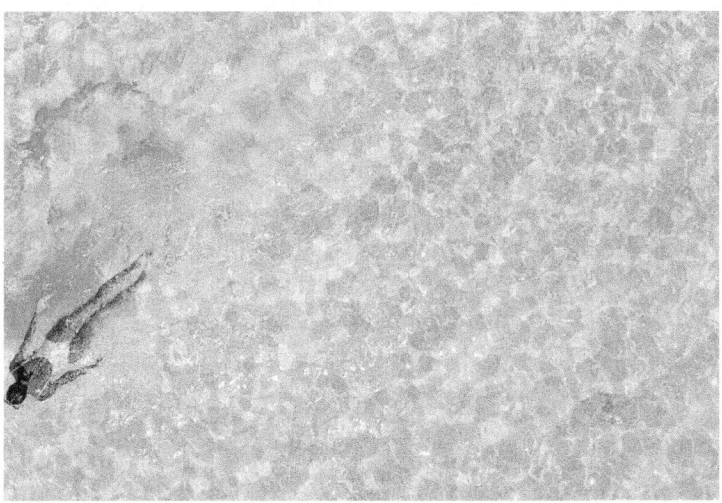

Hietaniemi Beach, popularly known as "Hietsu" among locals, is a popular and active urban beach located in Helsinki. Nestled along the Baltic Sea coastline, this sandy paradise gives both inhabitants and tourists a refreshing retreat from the city's hustle and bustle. Stretching over a kilometer, Hietaniemi Beach provides adequate room for guests to bask in the sun, relax, and enjoy the ocean. The beach features beautiful golden sand that's excellent for resting, building sandcastles, or indulging in a game of beach volleyball. The shallow waters near the shoreline are suitable for swimming, especially for families with young children. The beach is well-maintained, ensuring a comfortable and clean atmosphere for all.

One of the beach's main characteristics is its unique changing huts. These colorful, artistically painted cottages provide a bit of local culture to the beach and allow guests a spot to change into their swimwear and keep their stuff securely. The cabin rental system is a unique experience in itself, and the cabins are offered for a minimal cost.

For those wishing to enjoy more than simply a casual dip, Hietaniemi Beach provides various facilities and activities. Lifeguards are on duty during the summer months, safeguarding the safety of swimmers and offering peace of mind for families. The beach also contains floating docks in the ocean, creating dedicated spaces for diving and sunbathing surrounded by the relaxing sea.

After a refreshing plunge, beachgoers can explore the broad choice of food and beverage options nearby. From seaside shops providing ice cream and snacks to adjacent cafes and restaurants, there's something to suit every appetite. Visitors can taste local delights or foreign cuisine while taking in the breathtaking sea views.

Hietaniemi Beach is more than just a swimming destination; it's a hive of activity. It routinely hosts events and festivals, contributing to its dynamic vibe. Concerts, beach parties, and cultural festivals are hosted here, making it a bustling location that draws people from all walks of life. These activities provide a wonderful opportunity to connect with the local culture and make new acquaintances.

The beach's accessibility is another feature. Situated close to the city center, Hietaniemi Beach is easily accessed by public transit, bicycle, or even on foot. The simplicity of its position allows tourists to combine their beach days with other Helsinki attractions, such as the neighboring Seurasaari Open-Air Museum or a leisurely stroll through the lovely Töölönlahti Bay region.

However, it's worth mentioning that the water temperatures in the Baltic Sea may be extremely chilly, even during the summer months. While the Finnish sauna tradition is renowned, the inhabitants regularly rotate between the heat of the sauna and the refreshing waves of the sea, a practice that invigorates both body and mind.

Cruises and Boating

For travelers looking to discover Helsinki from a different perspective, engaging in cruises and boating adventures gives an unrivaled chance. The merging of Finland's rich maritime heritage with its contemporary metropolitan surroundings produces an experience that incorporates both cultural immersion and calm leisure.

Helsinki's waterfront serves as the gateway to a multitude of cruise alternatives that appeal to varied preferences. From leisurely sightseeing cruises to adventure-filled excursions, travelers can choose from a choice of vessels to set sail on. Many of these cruises travel the archipelago around the city, allowing visitors to view the spectacular natural splendor that defines the region. The archipelago encompasses thousands of islands, each sporting its own individual beauty, whether it's the calm of unspoiled landscapes or the vibrant local villages. Visitors can pick between narrated tours that provide historical background and insights into the city's past, or opt for more engaging experiences that include onboard activities, music, and entertainment.

For those who prefer a more intimate marine experience, boating is an attractive option. Helsinki provides chances for hiring rowboats, sailboats, and motorboats, enabling tourists to cruise the city's waterways at their own pace. The tranquil waters of Lake Saimaa, the largest lake in Finland, offer a peaceful environment for a day of sailing. Navigating the calm waves while being surrounded by the city's architecture may be a genuinely relaxing experience. Fishing enthusiasts can also cast their hooks into the Baltic Sea or the various lakes within and surrounding Helsinki, trying their luck at capturing native fish and contributing to the centuries-old Finnish fishing culture.

As the Finnish capital has expanded, so too has its maritime culture. Helsinki's waterfront region is a hive of activity, containing both modern conveniences and ancient landmarks. The UNESCO World Heritage-listed Suomenlinna Sea Fortress, located just a short ferry journey away from the city, is a prime example of this mix of history and modernity. The fortress, built in the 18th century, serves as a tribute to Finland's strategic significance and its storied past. Exploring its intricate tunnels, bastions, and museums offers a look into the nation's past while enjoying panoramic views of the sea.

Cruises and boating adventures in Helsinki are not just about leisure; they also provide insight into Finnish culture and traditions. The proximity to the Baltic Sea has generated a deep connection between the Finnish people and their nautical environment. This is visible in the city's maritime festivities, such as the Baltic Herring Fair, which celebrates the value of fishing to the local economy and highlights the culinary delights obtained from the sea. Tourists can mingle with locals during these festivities, acquiring a greater appreciation for the symbiotic link between the city and its seas.

Canoeing & Kayaking

Canoeing and kayaking offer a unique and immersive way to explore the gorgeous waterways of Helsinki, the capital city of Finland. Nestled between the Baltic Sea and many interconnecting lakes, Helsinki provides an ideal setting for water enthusiasts to explore the beauty of nature while having an exciting adventure.

Canoeing and kayaking are popular outdoor sports in Helsinki, allowing tourists to explore the city's natural grandeur from a different perspective. With its complicated network of aquatic features, including the Gulf of Finland, the Vantaa River, and other lakes, Helsinki begs travelers to embark on a tour that combines exercise, leisure, and sightseeing.

Equipment and Rentals
Tourists can easily obtain canoeing and kayaking equipment through rental services offered in and around the city. These businesses include several types of kayaks and canoes ideal for different ability levels, from beginners to experienced paddlers. Additionally, they offer safety gear, including life jackets and waterproof bags to secure personal items.

Top Canoeing/Kayaking Spots
Helsinki Archipelago: The archipelago is a dream for paddlers, with a tangle of islands, islets, and rugged coasts to explore. The calm seas and gorgeous vistas make it an amazing experience.

Nuuksio National Park: Nuuksio also offers tranquil lakes and pristine wilderness. Paddling through the quiet waters surrounded by beautiful woodlands is a refreshing experience.

Vantaa River: This River provides an opportunity to view the urban and natural landscapes of Helsinki in harmony. Paddlers can travel through the heart of the city, passing landmarks like the Helsinki Zoo and Seurasaari Open-Air Museum.

Laajalahti Bay: This bay is recognized for its rich wildlife and tranquil atmosphere. Paddlers can have a pleasant experience while seeing several bird species in their natural habitat.

Guided Tours and Safety
For those new to canoeing or kayaking, guided tours are a terrific way to explore the waters safely. Experienced guides accompany participants through pathways that emphasize the best of Helsinki's natural beauty while assuring their safety

throughout the tour. These trips generally include instructions on paddling techniques and safety precautions.

Seasonal Considerations
It's crucial to note that the greatest season for canoeing and kayaking in Helsinki is during the warmer months, often from late spring to early autumn. During this period, the weather is milder, water temperatures are more pleasant, and the scenery is at its most brilliant.

Environmental Responsibility
While enjoying the waterways, it's vital to practice responsible tourism. This involves respecting the local flora and fauna, abiding by established routes, and leaving no trace behind. By doing so, travelers can contribute to the preservation of Helsinki's natural assets.

Golf

Amidst this metropolitan attractiveness is a hidden gem for golf aficionados — a burgeoning golf scene that offers a great blend of sport and scenic beauty. With multiple well-maintained courses, magnificent surroundings, and a golf-friendly ambiance, Helsinki has also grown as a sought-after destination for both local and international golfers.

One of the primary factors that make golfing in Helsinki special is the stunning surroundings. The city features a stunning coastline setting with lush flora, tranquil water bodies, and a blend of urban and natural environments. Golf courses are intentionally constructed to combine with the existing beauty of the place. Keimola Golf, for instance, is set amidst forests and lakes, allowing golfers a chance to immerse themselves in nature while enjoying the game.

Helsinki's golfing season normally stretches from May to September, corresponding with the good weather of the region. During this period, golfers can take advantage of the long daylight hours to extend their fun well into the evening. This unique sensation of playing golf in the northern sun lends an added layer of appeal to the sport.

For beginners and novices, Helsinki offers a number of possibilities to get started with golf. Many courses give tuition for players of all ages and skill levels. This inclusivity has led to the growing popularity of the sport inside the city. Moreover, the calm and friendly attitude at Helsinki's golf clubs makes it simpler for newbies to feel accepted and encouraged to take up the game.

Travelers wishing to enjoy a golfing trip in Helsinki have various courses to choose from. Tapiola Golf, for example, is noted for its tough fairways and wonderfully crafted holes. Sea Golf Rönnäs, located approximately an hour's drive from the city center, offers spectacular sea vistas and different levels of difficulty across its 27 holes. The combination of varied courses ensures that golfers of all ability levels can find a fitting challenge.

Golfing in Helsinki is also a social affair. Many golf clubs offer cozy clubhouses where golfers may unwind after a game, enjoy native Finnish cuisine, and trade tales. This connection among golfers develops a sense of community and often leads to lifelong friendships.

It's worth mentioning that Helsinki's dedication to sustainability extends to its golf courses. Many of the golf courses prioritize ecologically friendly techniques, such as efficient water consumption, native plant landscaping, and eco-friendly maintenance. This technique not only boosts the aesthetic appeal of the courses but also corresponds with the city's greater ecological understanding.

In terms of logistics, Helsinki is well-equipped to welcome golf travelers. The city offers a choice of housing alternatives, from luxurious hotels to lovely boutique cottages. Public transportation is excellent, making it easy to commute between the city center and several golf courses.

Ice Skating

Helsinki transforms into a winter wonderland, offering a wealth of ice skating activities that appeal to skaters of all levels, from beginners to experts. With frozen lakes, well-maintained rinks, and a dash of Finnish flair, ice skating becomes an unforgettable hobby.

One of the delights of ice skating in Helsinki is the possibility of gliding across the frozen surface of natural lakes. During the colder months, lakes such as Töölönlahti and Kivinokka freeze over, creating enormous, glittering stretches of ice. These natural ice skating rinks are a distinctive element of Helsinki's winter landscape, giving skaters with an authentic and picturesque experience. The cold air, surrounded by snow-covered trees and the city's architecture in the distance, provides an environment that is both calm and thrilling.

For those searching for a more structured ice skating experience, Helsinki boasts a choice of well-maintained ice rinks. One of the most iconic is the Ice Park at the Railway Station Square. Set against the backdrop of the city's historic railway station, this outdoor rink offers a typical Finnish ice skating experience. The rink is meticulously manicured, giving a smooth surface for skaters to enjoy. Additionally, the Ice Park typically offers wonderful light displays and music, giving an air of enchantment to the skating session.

Another must-visit ice skating location is the Helsinki Ice Hall, which offers both recreational skating and ice hockey. This indoor arena provides a climate-controlled setting, making it a great choice for individuals who prefer to skate without suffering the chill of the outdoors. The Ice Hall also offers rental services, making it convenient for tourists who do not have their own ice skates.

For those looking to completely immerse themselves in the Finnish ice skating culture, taking part in the traditional saunaturns can be a unique experience. After a brisk skate, many people head to the sauna to warm up and relax. This age-old ritual is strongly embedded in Finnish culture and offers tourists a chance to participate in the native way of life.

Moreover, Helsinki's winter atmosphere extends beyond skating rinks. The city comes alive with festive markets, where tourists may sample local foods, and warm drinks, and browse for unique handicrafts. The Christmas markets, in particular, create an enchanting backdrop as skaters glide around the ice, surrounded by the sights and sounds of the holiday season.

Cross-country Skiing

This popular Nordic sport mixes physical activity with natural beauty, letting tourists explore the city's surroundings in a fresh and immersive way. Helsinki's winter beauty sets the stage for cross-country skiing enthusiasts. The city changes into a snowy wonderland, giving a stunning backdrop for outdoor activities. The dense network of parks, forests, and coastal areas provides a broad choice of skiing terrains, appropriate for both beginners and advanced skiers. Trails are often beautifully maintained, ensuring enjoyable skiing experiences. The Nuuksio National Park is a good place for skiing as well, with tracks that snake through frozen lakes, old woods, and rolling hills.

For travelers unfamiliar with cross-country skiing, Helsinki provides a choice of possibilities for instruction and rentals. Ski schools and sports centers provide instruction for all ability levels, making it easy for tourists to learn the basics of skiing skills and safety standards. Rentals are offered for individuals who choose not to invest in equipment for a short visit. This accessibility and assistance make the sport welcoming to folks of all ages and abilities.

One of the most enticing parts of cross-country skiing in Helsinki is the opportunity to enjoy the tranquility of nature. The serene forests and scenic pathways offer a peaceful getaway from the hustle and bustle of the city. As skiers glide over the snow-covered landscapes, they may get glimpses of local species and experience the calm splendor of Finland's winter wilderness.

The interconnecting path systems make it easy to explore various regions of the city and its surroundings. Skiers can embark on trips that take them from urban regions to more isolated locations, providing a unique perspective of Helsinki's different landscapes. The routes sometimes lead to attractive cafes and rest spots, allowing skiers to refuel and warm up while eating traditional Finnish cuisine and hot beverages.

Helsinki's winter weather can be hard, but it contributes to the realism of the cross-country skiing experience. Proper clothing and equipment are needed to keep comfortable in the chilly temperatures. Tourists are urged to dress in layers and wear moisture-wicking textiles to control body temperature. Additionally, wearing windproof and waterproof outer layers can defend against the elements.

Safety is a primary consideration, especially for individuals who are new to the sport. Skiers should be mindful of their own skill level and choose trails that match their abilities. It's also crucial to take things like a map, a fully charged phone, and a basic first aid kit. Staying hydrated and well-nourished is vital during skiing holidays, as physical exertion and low temperatures can boost calorie expenditure.

Conclusion
Helsinki stands as a paradise for outdoor enthusiasts, offering a varied choice of physical activities that allow travelers to immerse themselves in the city's natural splendor. From trekking in national parks to kayaking along the beach, the alternatives are as varied as they are compelling. Whether you're an adventure seeker, a nature lover, or someone who simply appreciates the outdoors, Helsinki's attractions are guaranteed to leave you with cherished memories and a profound appreciation for the city's unique balance of urban life and natural beauty.

Dialects and Language

The linguistic landscape of Helsinki is largely Finnish, with Swedish additionally possessing an official position due to the country's duality. Additionally, English is widely spoken and understood due to its role in international communication and tourism.

Finnish, known as "suomi" in the local tongue, is the major language spoken in Helsinki. It belongs to the Finno-Ugric language family, which is distinct from the Indo-European languages commonly spoken in many other parts of Europe. Finnish is noted for its complicated grammar and wide use of cases, which are grammatical elements that show the relationship between words in a phrase. This trait typically causes difficulty for non-native speakers, yet it is also part of what makes the language intriguing.

Swedish, referred to as "Svenska," is the second official language of Finland. This language effect can be traced back to Finland's historical ties with Sweden when the region was under Swedish rule. Today, roughly 5.5% of the population in Finland speak Swedish as their mother tongue, and this number is larger in cities like Helsinki. Street signs, government papers, and public services are commonly multilingual, reflecting the country's commitment to promoting both languages.

English has achieved tremendous popularity in Helsinki and throughout Finland due to its role as the lingua franca of international communication. Many Finns, especially the younger generation, are skilled in English, making it easier for travelers to traverse the city without linguistic obstacles.

Moreover, the education system in Finland places a significant focus on studying other languages, with English being the primary choice for most students.

Helsinki's linguistic diversity is further increased by the presence of diverse immigrant communities. The city has seen a surge in the number of people from varied linguistic backgrounds, including Russian, Estonian, and Somali speakers, among others. While these languages may not be as extensively spoken as Finnish, Swedish, or English, they add to the city's cosmopolitan fabric and offer visitors the opportunity to experience distinct linguistic and cultural nuances.

In terms of dialects, Helsinki's language landscape is typified by the Standard Finnish dialect, which is the most frequently recognized and used variety of the language. This dialect serves as the basis for education, media, and official communication. However, Finland is noted for its vast range of regional dialects, each with its own particular traits and subtleties. These dialects are frequently more popular in rural areas and smaller towns rather than in the urban setting of Helsinki.

Conclusion
Helsinki has a fascinating linguistic landscape with Finnish as the majority language, Swedish as a substantial minority language, and English as a universally essential communication tool. The city's history, school system, and foreign links have all had a role in establishing its diversified linguistic environment. While Finnish grammar and dialects could provide some obstacles, the abundance of English and the city's language-friendly environment make it a welcoming destination for travelers from throughout the world. Whether

you're exploring the local market, visiting cultural attractions, or simply navigating the city streets, you're sure to find a blend of languages that represents the cosmopolitan and linked nature of modern Helsinki.

Weather

A significant component of preparing a vacation to Helsinki is understanding its weather patterns, since they greatly influence the kind of activities you may enjoy and the clothing you should take. Helsinki features a moderate climate defined by different seasons. Each season has its own beauty and opportunity for exploration.

Winter (December - February)
Winter in Helsinki is a mesmerizing wonderland, as the city transforms into a magnificent setting with snow-covered streets and chilly scenery. The temperatures throughout these months frequently linger around -5°C to -10°C (23°F to 14°F), and occasionally drop lower. This is the time for experiencing traditional Finnish saunas and enjoying winter activities like ice skating and cross-country skiing.

Spring (March - May)
As the snow starts to melt and the days become longer, Helsinki sees a gentle transition into spring. Temperatures start to rise, ranging from 0°C to 10°C (32°F to 50°F). Spring is a time of regeneration, with locals emerging from winter hibernation to enjoy the blossoming parks and outdoor markets. It's also a fantastic time to explore cultural institutions and museums, as the weather is milder and more pleasant for walking excursions.

Summer (June - August)
Helsinki definitely comes alive during the summer months, with its typical temperatures ranging from 15°C to 25°C (59°F to 77°F). The city's numerous parks and waterfront areas become dynamic hubs for inhabitants and tourists alike. This

is the optimum season for open-air concerts, festivals, and leisurely boat trips to local islands. The famed "White Nights" phenomenon happens during this season, where the sun hardly sets, producing a unique and lovely environment.

Autumn (September - November)
Autumn paints Helsinki in rich shades of orange and gold as the leaves change color. The temperatures start to dip again, ranging from 5°C to 15°C (41°F to 59°F). This is a perfect time for nature enthusiasts to explore the city's surrounding forests and lakes, as well as enjoy the local harvest celebrations. The slightly cooler temperature also lends itself to exploring interior attractions like galleries and pleasant cafes.

It's crucial to realize that Helsinki's weather may be fairly changeable even within a single season. Rainfall is a typical occurrence throughout the year, therefore taking an umbrella and waterproof gear is essential. Additionally, the proximity of the city to the Baltic Sea can result in rapid temperature swings and sharp sea breezes, especially during the transitional months.

When packing for a vacation to Helsinki, it's advisable to have a varied wardrobe that includes layers. Regardless of the season, carrying essentials such as a waterproof jacket, suitable walking shoes, and warm clothing is a wise choice. Also, don't forget to pack swimsuits and light clothing for the summer, as well as snug winter attire for the colder months.

Conclusion
Understanding Helsinki's weather is important for a memorable and enjoyable vacation. The city's diverse seasons offer a multitude of activities and experiences, from winter sports to summer festivities. By arranging your trip

around the temperature and packing properly, you'll be well-prepared to immerse yourself in the beauty and culture of this delightful Finnish capital.

Getting Here

This section offers a full description of how to reach this picturesque city, covering transit alternatives, essential travel hubs, and advice to make your journey a pleasant one.

By Air
Helsinki-Vantaa Airport (HEL) is the principal gateway for international travelers. It is well-connected to major cities across the globe and offers a wealth of services, making it a handy starting place for your journey. From the airport, you may easily reach the city center utilizing numerous transit modes such as trains, buses, and taxis. The trek takes roughly 30 minutes and provides a peek at the Finnish environment.

By Train
Helsinki is well-connected to neighboring nations via an efficient railway network. The Allegro high-speed train connects Helsinki to St. Petersburg, Russia, in around 3.5 hours, giving a magnificent ride through woods and lakes. Additionally, the popular Santa Claus Express connects Helsinki to Rovaniemi, the official hometown of Santa Claus, in roughly 8 hours. Comfortable cabins make overnight journeys a comfortable alternative.

By Sea
For a unique experience, consider arriving in Helsinki by ferry. The city boasts a lively harbor that connects it to Tallinn, Estonia, and Stockholm, Sweden. The overnight ferries provide a luxurious yet economical form of transportation, replete with cabins, restaurants, and entertainment options.

The ride gives stunning views of the archipelago as you approach the Finnish coastline.

By Bus
If you're going within Europe, long-distance buses offer a cost-effective option to reach Helsinki. The vast road network offers good connectivity, and the buses are noted for their comfort and convenience. They often provide vital conveniences such as Wi-Fi and power outlets, making travel comfortable.

By Car
For those seeking flexibility, renting a car can be an option worth exploring. Finland's well-maintained road system guarantees a smooth driving experience. However, bear in mind that driving conditions can be hard during the winter months, so be prepared with adequate winter tires and equipment.

Local Transportation
Upon arriving in Helsinki, you'll find an excellent public transit system consisting of trams, buses, and the metro. The city is recognized for its walkability, thus exploring on foot is highly recommended. To make your trips even simpler, consider getting a Helsinki Card, which allows unrestricted access to public transport as well as free admittance to various museums and sites.

Conclusion
Helsinki offers a wide choice of transportation options to suit diverse interests and budgets. Whether you're arriving by air, rail, boat, bus, or vehicle, the city's superb connectivity ensures hassle-free travel. Remember to verify visa requirements, embrace the local transit system, and immerse

yourself in the enchanting culture of this Nordic treasure. Your adventure in Helsinki begins the moment you get into your chosen form of transportation, ensuring a memorable encounter from start to finish.

Top Attractions

With a rich history reaching back to the 16th century, Helsinki has evolved into a lively cultural city that provides an array of tourist attractions for every style of traveler. From its stunning architecture to its tranquil natural landscapes, Helsinki provides a memorable experience that combines history, culture, and modern urban living. Here are the popular tourist attractions in Helsinki:

Suomenlinna Fortress

Suomenlinna Fortress, as described earlier is located on a collection of islands off the coast of Helsinki, it is a mesmerizing historical landmark that allows visitors an insight into the nation's past. This UNESCO World Heritage-listed landmark is not only a famous tourist destination but also a symbol of Finland's rich history, architectural prowess, and geopolitical significance. With its captivating blend of military architecture, spectacular natural settings, and cultural attractions, Suomenlinna stands as a witness to Finland's growth through the centuries.

Originally erected in the mid-18th century, Suomenlinna was designed as a naval fortress by the Swedish monarch to secure its interests in the Baltic Sea region. The fortress's location spread across six interconnecting islands, offered it a strategic edge in securing naval routes and commercial routes. The architectural layout exhibits a blend of medieval fortifications and modern bastions, illustrating the history of defensive systems. The fort's name, meaning "Castle of Finland," accurately expresses its role as a defender of the nation's coastal waters.

As history developed, Suomenlinna shifted hands from the Swedes to the Russians in the early 19th century, following Finland's annexation by the Russian Empire. During this period, the castle experienced extensive improvements, with the construction of additional barracks, defensive fortifications, and even a naval facility. However, the early 20th century saw Finland earn its independence, beginning a new chapter for the nation and the castle. Today, Suomenlinna is a harmonic blend of many cultural influences, including Finnish, Swedish, and Russian heritage.

One of the most outstanding elements of Suomenlinna is its architectural diversity. Visitors can explore a profusion of structures, including defensive walls, tunnels, gates, and artillery emplacements. The King's Gate embellished with a spectacular lion sculpture, and the Great Courtyard, where the heart of the fortress sits, are must-see sights. The fortifications not only served military functions but also formed a self-sufficient village, complete with houses, businesses, and even a chapel. The relics of this settlement offer a look into daily life within the fortification.

Beyond its military heritage, Suomenlinna offers a range of cultural activities that cater to varied interests. The Suomenlinna Museum, based in the Commander's House, chronicles the fortress's history through exhibitions, artifacts, and interactive displays. The Toy Museum shows a lovely collection of toys, giving insight into childhood experiences through the decades. Art galleries and workshops are distributed around the islands, offering a platform for contemporary artists to display their creations.

However, it's not simply the historical significance and cultural attractions that lure visitors to Suomenlinna; the natural beauty of the islands is as enchanting. Verdant parks, peaceful waterfronts, and panoramic overlooks offer an idyllic atmosphere for relaxation and exploration. The sea wind, coupled with the sound of lapping waves, adds to the peacefulness of the experience.

Helsinki Cathedral

Helsinki Cathedral, also known as Tuomiokirkko in Finnish, stands as an iconic symbol of Finnish architecture, culture, and history. Located in the center of Helsinki, this neoclassical masterpiece is a notable landmark that attracts both tourists and locals alike.

Designed by the eminent architect Carl Ludvig Engel, the Helsinki Cathedral's construction began in 1830 and was completed in 1852, a witness to the exquisite attention to detail and dedication to design that was characteristic of the era. The cathedral's grandeur is a reflection of Engel's influence, as well as the neoclassical architectural movement that was prevalent in the early 19th century.

The exterior of the Helsinki Cathedral offers a stunning presence with its spotless white façade, crowned by a succession of green domes and a central dome that rises beautifully into the skyline. The cathedral's design draws inspiration from ancient Greek and Roman architecture, as seen in its symmetrical arrangement, beautiful columns, and pediments. The exquisite sculptures and reliefs that adorn the outside pay homage to Finnish history, culture, and religion, encapsulating a feeling of national identity inside the architectural masterpiece.

As guests go inside the cathedral, they are met by a spacious and airy interior that shows a blend of simplicity and beauty. The lofty ceilings, embellished with beautiful frescoes, generate a sense of awe and devotion. The enormous altar, bathed in soft light, serves as the focal center of the interior, while the superb pulpit and organ further enhance the cathedral's spiritual aura.

One of the most outstanding elements of the Helsinki Cathedral is its collection of exquisite artwork and religious symbols. The exquisite stained glass windows, constructed by Engel's students, allow colorful light to filter into the inside, creating a tranquil atmosphere for thought and contemplation. The cathedral holds various statues and sculptures, including the twelve apostles, each a fine example of Finnish craftsmanship and commitment to artistic detail.

The cathedral's impact on Finnish society extends beyond its architectural significance. It has witnessed key historical events, from royal celebrations to the nation's proclamation of independence in 1917. Its central placement in Senate Square has made it a gathering center for both solemn occasions and exuberant festivals, further embedding it into the cultural fabric of Helsinki.

For travelers seeking a deeper understanding of Finnish history and theology, guided tours of the cathedral are given. Knowledgeable guides provide insights into the architectural intricacies, historical background, and religious relevance of the cathedral. Visitors can learn about the importance of the Finnish Evangelical Lutheran Church, to which the cathedral belongs, and its influence on the country's identity.

Furthermore, the Helsinki Cathedral's surrounds add to its charm. The Senate Square, built by Engel as well, has well-preserved neoclassical structures and a statue of Alexander II, the Russian Emperor who launched the construction of the cathedral. The square's wide expanse allows for diverse events and festivities, making it a dynamic center throughout the year.

Uspenski Cathedral

The Uspenski Cathedral, a magnificent Orthodox cathedral, serves as an iconic tribute to both architectural grandeur and cultural relevance. This cathedral, built atop a hill overlooking the city and the harbor, offers an awe-inspiring blend of history, art, and spirituality.

Completed in 1868, the Uspenski Cathedral is not only the largest Orthodox cathedral in Western Europe but also one of the most spectacular specimens of Russian Revival architecture. Its unique red brick façade, decorated with delicate white brickwork, captures quick notice and contrasts well against the surrounding vegetation and turquoise seas. The cathedral's design was influenced by Byzantine architecture, as seen in its onion-shaped domes which are a trademark of Orthodox churches. These domes are covered in gleaming gold leaf, which catches the sunlight and produces a magnificent visual spectacle.

Beyond its architectural magnificence, the Uspenski Cathedral possesses great cultural and theological significance. It is a symbol of Finland's historical relationship with Russia, as the country was under Russian administration when the cathedral was erected. The cathedral is dedicated to the Assumption of Mary and serves as the major cathedral of the Finnish Orthodox Church. Inside, guests are met by an atmosphere of reverence and tranquillity. The inside is filled with bright frescoes, complex iconostases, and beautiful chandeliers, providing a sense of richness and devotion. The icons show scenes from the life of Christ and numerous saints, contributing to the spiritual aura of the room.

One of the cathedral's most notable aspects is its collection of sacred items. The Uspenski Cathedral has an array of rare icons, chalices, and vestments that offer a look into the rich history of Orthodox Christianity. Many of these artifacts are elegantly embellished with precious metals and gemstones, demonstrating the skill and artistry of artists over the ages. Visitors get the opportunity to learn about the significance of these objects and their role in Orthodox worship.

The cathedral's location atop a hill affords panoramic views of Helsinki, adding to its attractiveness for tourists. As tourists ascend the steps to the cathedral, they are treated to breathtaking perspectives of the city's cityscape, the port, and the Baltic Sea. This vantage position is particularly intriguing during sunset, as the departing light spreads a warm glow over the cityscape, producing a genuinely spectacular experience.

For those eager to dig deeper into the history and spirituality of the Uspenski Cathedral, guided tours are provided.

Knowledgeable interpreters provide engaging anecdotes about the cathedral's construction, its importance in Finnish history, and the Orthodox faith. These tours typically provide insights into the practices and traditions associated with Orthodox prayer, helping visitors to comprehend the spiritual significance of the site.

Temppeliaukio Church (Rock Church)

Temppeliaukio Church, often known as the Rock Church, is a remarkable architectural masterpiece. This extraordinary place of worship, developed by architects Timo and Tuomo Suomalainen, is a prime example of inventive design that flawlessly mixes nature and modern construction techniques.

Built straight into solid rock, the Temppeliaukio Church is a tribute to human inventiveness and the harmonious coexistence of man-made structures with the natural surroundings. The church's appearance is inconspicuous, with only a copper dome and stone walls visible above ground. However, the actual marvel lurks beneath the surface. A substantial piece of the church is hewn out of solid bedrock, providing a calm sanctuary that seems to erupt from the earth itself.

Upon entering the church, guests are welcomed by an awe-inspiring scene. The natural light coming in through the glass dome lights the rock walls, creating a tranquil and ethereal ambiance. The interior is distinguished by a minimalist design that accentuates the organic shapes and textures of the stone walls. The craggy rock surfaces serve as a stunning backdrop for numerous events, such as concerts and weddings, making the area adaptable and culturally vibrant.

One of the most outstanding characteristics of the Temppeliaukio Church is its extraordinary acoustics. The natural qualities of the granite increase sound, offering a unique auditory experience for musical performances. As a result, the cathedral has become a sought-after location for classical and contemporary events, attracting music fans from around the world. The mix of the remarkable acoustics and the serene settings transforms each concert into a captivating spectacle.

The church's design not only stresses its relationship with nature but also showcases the creative approach to building. The use of modern building methods allowed the architects to create a usable space while conserving the integrity of the natural rock formations. This blend of ingenuity and environmental sensitivity has gained the Temppeliaukio Church great acclaim and status as a UNESCO World Heritage Site.

The religious and cultural significance of the church is another factor that fascinates tourists and locals alike. The church is used for religious services by the local Lutheran community, but its warm and inclusive ambiance also makes it a venue for individuals of all faiths to ponder and find solace. The spiritual air of the church, combined with its appealing design, provides a sense of unity that transcends religious bounds.

Surrounding the Temppeliaukio Church is a wonderful garden area that complements the overall experience. Visitors can enjoy a leisurely stroll amidst lush foliage, allowing for a period of contemplation before or after seeing the church's interior. The garden area also provides a great vantage point to view the unique architectural characteristics of the building's exterior, notably the copper dome that adds a touch of modern elegance to the natural setting.

Seurasaari Open-Air Museum

The Seurasaari Open-Air Museum acts as a living witness to Finland's rich cultural history and rural traditions. This unique museum provides visitors with a mesmerizing voyage back in time, allowing them to immerse themselves in the real charm of Finnish rural life from ages ago.

Spread across a lovely island, the Seurasaari Open-Air Museum is more than just a collection of antiquities; it's an experience window into the past. The museum's principal purpose is to preserve and highlight the unique architectural styles, cultural practices, and daily routines of Finland's rural towns. This is achieved by the meticulous reconstruction of over 80 historic buildings that have been meticulously transferred from different regions of the country to the island.

Visitors to the museum are greeted by a stunning assortment of farmhouses, cottages, and outbuildings, each expertly restored to its original state. These constructions span multiple ages, allowing a view into the developing architectural ideas and building techniques that influenced Finland's rural landscape. As you travel along the roads that wind through the island's lush landscapes, you'll discover residences that range from the 18th to the 20th century, allowing you to experience firsthand the growth of Finnish rural life.

What sets the Seurasaari Open-Air Museum distinctive is its devotion to authenticity. The interiors of these buildings are outfitted with period-appropriate things, from furniture to utensils, allowing a thorough knowledge of how people lived, worked, and interacted over different times. This attention to detail produces an immersive experience that transports visitors to a bygone period, producing a sense of nostalgia and awe.

Throughout the year, the museum presents a variety of activities and exhibitions that provide a deeper insight into Finland's cultural legacy. From traditional craft workshops to seasonal festivals, these programs provide visitors a chance to engage with history in a hands-on and meaningful way. The

Midsummer festivities, for example, allow visitors to join in the colorful rites and customs associated with this major Finnish event.

For those with a predilection for Finnish mythology and storytelling, the Seurasaari Open-Air Museum is a treasure mine. The guides and staff members are well-versed in the myths and traditions of the region, giving an extra element of magic to the guest experience. They may regale you with stories of legendary creatures, ancient beliefs, and the age-old traditions that have shaped the cultural fabric of Finland.

Sibelius Monument

The Sibelius Monument is a beautiful memorial to the legendary Finnish composer, Jean Sibelius. Erected in 1967, this remarkable monument retains great cultural and artistic relevance within the country. Designed by Eila Hiltunen, a famous Finnish sculptor, the monument reflects the essence of Sibelius's music and soul.

Standing in Sibelius Park, the monument's abstract and futuristic style immediately draws attention. Comprising a network of 600 hollow steel pipes welded together, the sculpture stands an astonishing 8.5 meters in height. These pipes, organically flowing and resembling organ pipes, evoke the lovely sounds of Sibelius's compositions. The monument's open structure and the way it interacts with natural light and surroundings offer an immersive experience, representing the composer's ability to merge his music with the beauty of nature.

The monument's creation also carries symbolic importance. The hundreds of pipes reflect the trees of Finland's forests, which have long been a source of inspiration for Sibelius's music. The fluid lines of the pipes portray the organic flow of sound, capturing the dynamic and emotional spectrum contained in the composer's symphonies. This relationship between nature, music, and human creativity resonates with the core of Sibelius's work, making the monument not merely a portrayal of his image, but a manifestation of his artistic philosophy.

As people approach the monument, they often find themselves surrounded by an audio experience as well. Visitors are encouraged to engage with the sculpture by tapping on the pipes, producing musical tones that echo across the park. This interactive feature converts the site into a participatory art project, encouraging users to engage with Sibelius's melodies in a unique and physical way. This integration of visual and audio elements generates a multimodal interaction that increases one's connection to both the composer and his homeland.

While the Sibelius Monument is a testimony to the composer's enduring influence, it also acts as a reflection of Finland's national identity. Jean Sibelius is considered one of Finland's greatest cultural figures, and his compositions have played a crucial part in establishing the country's sense of self. The monument, thus, becomes not merely a memorial to the composer but also an expression of national pride and artistic excellence.

For those wanting a thorough experience, the adjacent Sibelius Park adds another dimension of investigation. The quiet ambiance, with abundant foliage and well-maintained pathways, provides a peaceful environment for contemplation and relaxation. The park's environment is in accord with the monument's aesthetic expression, emphasizing the connection between human creativity and the natural world.

Ateneum Art Museum

The museum's architecture itself is a work of art. Designed by Theophil von Hansen and finished in 1887, the edifice emanates neoclassical grandeur, standing as a tribute to the country's rich past and its respect for art. Its facade has exquisite details and columns that harken back to ancient Greek and Roman architectural influences. The majestic façade gives an appropriate introduction to the treasures contained within.

Upon entering the Ateneum, visitors are greeted by a broad and extensive collection of Finnish art spanning several centuries. The museum's principal focus lies on the 19th and 20th centuries, illustrating the evolution of Finnish artistic expression throughout a significant period in the nation's history. The collection contains paintings, sculptures, sketches, and prints, allowing visitors to trace the evolution of Finnish art via many mediums and styles.

One of the notable aspects of the Ateneum is its collection of paintings by prominent Finnish painters, including Albert Edelfelt, Akseli Gallen-Kallela, and Helene Schjerfbeck. These artists played significant roles in shaping Finnish art and are acknowledged for their contributions to both national and international aesthetic discourse. Their works offer insights into the cultural and social circumstances of their times, providing visitors with a fuller understanding of Finland's history and identity.

The museum's curatorial efforts extend beyond its permanent collection. The Ateneum frequently holds temporary exhibitions that explore numerous themes and artistic movements. These shows not only present fresh perspectives on Finnish art but also showcase international artists, promoting a cross-cultural discourse that improves the museum's offerings.

Education is at the center of the Ateneum's goal. The museum offers various educational programs, workshops, and guided tours that cater to guests of all ages. These projects engage visitors in participatory and thought-provoking ways, boosting their love of art and cultivating a lifetime relationship with creativity and culture.

In addition to its role as an artistic and educational center, the Ateneum acts as a forum for intellectual inquiry and artistic collaboration. The museum's library and archive house a significant collection of records, publications, and materials linked to Finnish art, providing researchers and art aficionados with important tools for further discovery and study.

The Ateneum Art Museum is not only a repository of artistic riches but also a reflection of Finland's artistic character. It encapsulates the nation's path from its identity-forming moments to its present artistic expressions, all within the confines of an architecturally noteworthy edifice. As a location that stimulates debate, reflection, and inspiration, the museum brings together individuals from all backgrounds to share in the beauty and power of art.

National Museum of Finland

Established in 1916, the National Museum is not only a cultural institution but also an architectural masterpiece. Designed by architect Herman Gesellius, the building shows a blend of national romanticism and medieval influences, typified by its red brick façade, decorative turrets, and intricate sculptures. This design philosophy mirrors the broader attitude of the time when Finland was expressing its national identity during the period of Russian control.

As guests go into the museum, they are met by a comprehensive display that covers prehistoric times to the current era. The Prehistory of Finland section digs into the Stone Age, Bronze Age, and Iron Age, exhibiting objects such as tools, swords, and jewelry that provide insight into the lives of ancient Finns. The museum's large collection of archaeological discoveries allows visitors to appreciate the evolution of human presence in the region.

Moving forward in time, the medieval phase uncovers Finland's relationships with surrounding cultures and the effect of Christianity. Exhibits include finely carved wooden altarpieces, religious artifacts, and things that demonstrate the relationship between Eastern and Western traditions. This part gives a vivid picture of Finland's path from paganism to a Christianized civilization.

The museum's crown gem, the "Finnish National Epic" show, commemorates the nation's literary heritage. It highlights the Kalevala, a 19th-century book created by Elias Lönnrot that weaves together Finnish folklore and mythology. Visitors are introduced to the epic's heroes, mythical creatures, and the spirit of national awakening that it embodied. This exhibit is a monument to the power of literature in forming a communal identity.

The National Museum doesn't shy away from confronting Finland's more volatile eras. The "100 Years of Finnish Independence" section goes into the nation's battle for autonomy, from its declaration of independence in 1917 through its emergence as a contemporary European state. The exhibitions represent the struggles, successes, and sacrifices made by the Finnish people during this historic period.

Art fans will admire the museum's extensive collection of Finnish visual art, including works from prominent painters like Akseli Gallen-Kallela and Helene Schjerfbeck. These pieces represent the progression of Finnish art, from its romantic roots to more current expressions. The juxtaposition of historical events with creative trends offers a holistic understanding of Finnish culture.

The National Museum's commitment to interactive and educational experiences is reflected in its digital installations and temporary exhibitions. These new features provide visitors with a fresh perspective on historical events and cultural phenomena. Through virtual reconstructions, immersive displays, and multimedia presentations, the museum bridges the gap between the past and the present, appealing to a varied variety of visitors.

Kiasma Museum of Contemporary Art

Designed by the American architect Steven Holl and opened in 1998, the museum acts as a focal point for modern art fans. At the heart of Kiasma's charm lies its unusual architectural design. The building's unusual construction is defined by a succession of bending curves and angles that perfectly merge into the urban surroundings. The use of materials such as glass, steel, and wood not only adds to its visual appeal but also allows for a harmonious interplay between the museum's internal and external spaces. The architecture itself invites visitors to explore its nooks and corners, making the journey through the museum as intriguing as the art it displays.

The museum's shows are a reflection of the ever-evolving world of contemporary art. Kiasma features a dynamic collection of Finnish and international artworks, covering many disciplines like painting, sculpture, photography, video art, and interactive installations. These shows often challenge conventional beliefs, inviting spectators to question and contemplate the themes offered. The rotating exhibitions ensure that each visit to Kiasma gives a fresh perspective, giving it a place that warrants multiple excursions.

What sets Kiasma distinct is its commitment to creating debate and engagement between art, artists, and the audience. The museum hosts a wide assortment of activities including workshops, lectures, and performances, creating a stimulating setting where visitors may engage directly with the creative process. Kiasma's emphasis on accessibility is reflected in its efforts to serve varied audiences, including children, students, and others with varying levels of experience with modern art. The outcome is an inclusive arena that demystifies art and invites everyone to engage in the debate.

The Kiasma Museum of Contemporary Art also functions as a cultural center for Helsinki and beyond. Its strategic location in the city center makes it easily accessible to both locals and tourists, and its involvement in hosting international exhibitions and collaborations helps Finland's standing on the world art scene. The museum's building alone has become an iconic landmark, gathering enthusiasts of design and culture alike.

A visit to Kiasma is an engaging experience that engages all the senses. The interaction between light and space, the juxtaposition of artworks, and the meticulously organized displays create a narrative that inspires thought and meditation. Whether one is an art aficionado or a novice, Kiasma offers an environment where personal interpretations and emotional responses are not only encouraged but celebrated.

Esplanade Park

Stretching between two major streets, Mannerheimintie and Pohjoisesplanadi, this historic park has long been a favorite gathering spot for both locals and tourists alike. Spanning an area of nearly 21,000 square meters, Esplanade Park features a rich history, gorgeous flora, and a plethora of cultural events.

Originally envisaged in the early 19th century, Esplanade Park has experienced several alterations that have created its contemporary personality. The park's design was greatly influenced by the principles of Romanticism, which aspired to create natural and beautiful areas within urban contexts. As a result, tourists now can meander through tree-lined pathways, view the elaborate sculptures and fountains, and relax on the well-maintained lawns. The park's design perfectly mixes nature and art, creating a refuge of peace inside the city's lively center.

One of the park's defining features is its collection of beautiful statues and monuments, each with its own narrative to tell. The Johan Ludvig Runeberg monument, dedicated to Finland's national poet, is a landmark, reflecting the country's great admiration for its cultural legacy. Another prominent sculpture is the Havis Amanda fountain, which has become an iconic emblem of Helsinki. This exquisite statue depicts a mermaid rising from the sea, reflecting the city's link to the Baltic Sea and its maritime past.

Esplanade Park also plays a vital part in Helsinki's cultural scene. Throughout the year, the park holds many events and performances that interest both locals and visitors. From summer concerts and open-air theatre to art exhibitions and food festivals, the park has become a dynamic center of activity. Its central location makes it a great spot to unwind and enjoy entertainment in a lovely environment.

Moreover, the park's surrounding neighborhood is lined with attractive stores, cafes, and restaurants that offer a blend of local and international food. Many people take advantage of this juxtaposition, enjoying leisurely strolls across the park before or after a full supper. The setting becomes particularly charming during the summer months when the park's trees are in full bloom and the outside terraces are abuzz with diners relishing the ambiance.

Esplanade Park's historical significance also makes it a destination of cultural and architectural interest. The park is flanked by buildings that demonstrate many architectural styles, from neoclassical façade to more modern designs. These structures serve as a visual chronology of Helsinki's growth and contribute to the park's unique character.

Design Museum Helsinki

Design Museum Helsinki is a cultural gem that highlights the country's rich design legacy and its contributions to worldwide design innovation. Established in 1873, the museum has evolved over the years to become a lively institution that celebrates and educates visitors about the wide world of design.

The museum's architecture itself is a masterpiece, with a combination of antique and modern components that harmoniously integrate into the urban setting. Its facade is a blend of Art Nouveau and contemporary style, producing an intriguing juxtaposition that provokes curiosity before ever entering the museum. This distinctive architectural style sets the tone for what visitors may expect inside a voyage through time and space exploring the domains of Finnish and international design.

Inside, the Design Museum Helsinki provides an enormous collection of over 75,000 pieces that span numerous design disciplines, including industrial design, fashion, textiles, graphic design, and more. From classic pieces of Finnish furniture to avant-garde fashion items, the museum's exhibitions offer a thorough picture of design evolution over the decades.

One of the museum's significant features is its concentration on Finnish design, which has garnered a global reputation for its simple aesthetics, functionality, and connection to nature. Visitors have the opportunity to dig into the roots of renowned Finnish design businesses like Marimekko and Artek, which have made an unmistakable influence on the international design scene. The museum takes visitors on a trip through major events in Finnish design history, showing the relationship between tradition and innovation.

While the Design Museum Helsinki acknowledges its national design past, it also underlines the importance of international design exchange. Temporary exhibitions regularly incorporate collaborations with design institutions from throughout the world, giving fresh insights and cross-cultural influences to its viewers. This method not only maintains the museum current and relevant but also encourages a global design discussion.

The Design Museum also offers a range of educational programs and activities. Workshops, talks, and guided tours give visitors deeper insights into the design process and its impact on society. The museum's focus on teaching extends to younger audiences as well, with interactive events aimed to stimulate creativity and a love for design in children and teens.

The Design Museum Helsinki also serves as a forum for researching the convergence of design, technology, and sustainability. With the ever-growing emphasis on environmental consciousness, the museum routinely offers exhibitions and conversations that highlight the role of design in crafting a more sustainable future. These exhibits demonstrate breakthrough materials, eco-friendly techniques, and design solutions that solve modern global concerns.

As visitors explore the museum's displays, they are asked to reflect on the importance of design in influencing our daily lives. From the chairs we sit on to the clothes we wear, design shapes our experiences in ways we often take for granted. The Design Museum Helsinki encourages visitors to investigate the stories behind common products and how design decisions affect usefulness, aesthetics, and even emotions.

Helsinki Zoo

Also known as "Korkeasaari," created in 1889, Helsinki Zoo has evolved from a modest collection of animals into a sophisticated conservation institution, dedicated to the welfare of its inhabitants and the preservation of endangered species. The zoo's strategic placement on an island guarantees a realistic environment, allowing animals to inhabit enclosures that closely imitate their native environments. Visitors are thus exposed to a seamless blend of instruction and enjoyment.

One of the zoo's main characteristics is its thematic displays that take visitors to different corners of the globe. From the Arctic tundra to the African savannah, each enclosure is carefully constructed to resemble the animals' native surroundings. The "Big Cat Valley" is a prime example, allowing a glimpse into the worlds of beautiful predators like lions, tigers, and snow leopards. The "Amazonia" section immerses visitors in the South American rainforests, which are home to exotic birds, monkeys, and jaguars. The Helsinki Zoo raises visitors' knowledge of a variety of species and the value of maintaining their natural habitats through these exhibits.

Beyond its status as a leisure spot, the zoo takes its conservation initiatives seriously. Participating in international breeding initiatives, the zoo contributes to protecting endangered species from around the world. Its involvement in research and breeding activities for the European endangered species helps considerably to worldwide conservation efforts. By presenting these rare and endangered animals, the zoo develops a sense of responsibility among visitors, inspiring them to become champions for wildlife conservation.

Moreover, Helsinki Zoo's devotion to education is obvious through its varied programs and events. The "Zoo School" concept engages children in interactive learning experiences, educating them about biodiversity, ecosystems, and animal behavior. The zoo's outreach goes outside its borders, engaging with schools and organizations to promote environmental awareness and conservation.

In recent years, Helsinki Zoo has also embraced modern principles of animal welfare. Enclosures are created with a focus on enrichment, giving animals with mental and physical stimuli to replicate their natural habits. Ethical considerations have led to the establishment of more spacious and fascinating surroundings, assuring the well-being of the animals while enriching the tourist experience.

The experience at Helsinki Zoo is not confined to animal exhibitions alone. The zoo offers a number of attractions, including guided tours, family-friendly activities, and restaurants providing locally sourced cuisine. Visitors can embark on a guided tour to acquire greater insights into the animals' lives, behaviors, and the zoo's conservation initiatives. The "Zoo by Night" program provides a unique opportunity to view nocturnal animals in their element, presenting a fresh perspective on the animal kingdom.

Linnanmäki Amusement Park

Linnanmäki Amusement Park's history stretches back to its creation in 1950, offering a broad choice of attractions, stunning rides, and an unbroken commitment to family pleasure, Linnanmäki retains a particular place in the hearts of all who visit.

Upon entering Linnanmäki, visitors are met with a lively and colorful ambiance that instantly sets the setting for an amazing encounter. The park's layout is cleverly constructed, allowing for easy navigation while creating a sense of anticipation as one explores its numerous themed regions. From the moment one steps through the entrance gate, the sights, sounds, and aromas of excitement flood the air, promising a day of sheer delight.

A characteristic of Linnanmäki is its broad array of rides that cater to individuals of all ages. Adrenaline junkies are sure to be pleased by the towering roller coasters that feature heart-pounding dips, inversions, and speeds that will leave them breathless. For families with younger children, the park's collection of moderate rides gives a more calm yet equally entertaining experience. From spinning teacups to quirky carousels, there's something for everyone to enjoy.

One of the park's major features is the renowned "Linnunrata" roller coaster, a real classic that has captured the hearts of generations. This wooden coaster, first built in 1951, is not simply a ride; it's a tribute to the continuing charm of traditional amusement park attractions. As passengers soar into the air and handle tight bends, they're taken back to a simpler time, generating a unique blend of nostalgia and adrenaline.

Beyond the excitement of the rides, Linnanmäki is committed to providing a full entertainment experience. The park frequently presents intriguing live concerts, musical performances, and theatrical productions that lend an added degree of enchantment to the visit. These performances exhibit the abilities of local artists and entertainers, highlighting Finland's rich cultural legacy while keeping tourists involved and delighted.

A visit to Linnanmäki wouldn't be complete without indulging in its culinary options. The park features a variety of dining options, ranging from traditional Finnish delights to international cuisines. The food at Linnanmäki is as varied as the attractions, catering to a wide range of tastes and preferences, whether it's relishing a savory crepe, savoring a tasty burger, or satisfying a sweet appetite with cotton candy.

As a socially responsible vacation spot, Linnanmäki also takes pleasure in its commitment to helping philanthropic organizations. The park operates under the Children's Day Foundation, which contributes a portion of its income to groups dedicated to improving the lives of children in need. This altruistic mentality adds a touching depth to the park's appeal, allowing visitors to enjoy their time while donating to a great cause.

Museum of Finnish Architecture

Founded in 1956, and housed within a stunning building itself, the museum's architecture serves as an excellent introduction to the riches it possesses. Designed by architects Woldemar Baeckman and Gösta Juslén, the edifice effortlessly integrates neoclassical and functionalist features, representing the numerous architectural influences that have affected Finnish design through the years.

The museum's exhibitions are painstakingly curated to present a complete picture of Finnish architecture's history. The permanent collection displays an array of scale models, sketches, photographs, and other objects that trace the country's architectural history. It pays respect to old wooden structures, highlighting the workmanship that distinguished rural and urban environments before the arrival of modern construction processes.

One of the museum's notable attractions is its coverage of the "Golden Age" of Finnish architecture, which arose in the early 20th century. Architects such as Eliel Saarinen and Alvar Aalto acquired international fame for their creative designs, perfectly blending usefulness and aesthetics. Visitors can marvel at historic monuments like the Helsinki Central Railway Station, defined by its distinctive granite exterior and elaborate design features.

Continuing its narrative, the museum also dives into the post-World War II period when Finland witnessed significant urbanization and societal transformation. This era brought forth the birth of modernism, which substantially affected Finnish architectural ideas. Visitors can examine how architects like Aarno Ruusuvuori and Reima Pietilä adopted modernist concepts while adopting a particularly Finnish perspective, often harmonizing their designs with the natural landscape.

Moving forward in time, the museum's contemporary exhibitions highlight the bold experimentation and worldwide collaboration that define contemporary Finnish architecture. Sustainability, simplicity, and cutting-edge technology take center stage as architects push the boundaries of design while keeping cultural and environmental settings in mind.

The Museum of Finnish Architecture also presents rotating exhibitions that confront important issues and highlight architectural achievements both in Finland and beyond. Interactive displays and immersive experiences further engage visitors, giving a better awareness of the discipline's subtleties and relevance in influencing our surroundings.

The museum also works as a forum for architectural discourse and education. Lectures, workshops, and guided tours allow visitors the opportunity to engage with professionals and acquire insights into architectural theory, practice, and innovation. This emphasis on teaching emphasizes the institution's commitment to not only preserving the past but also inspiring the builders and designers of the future.

As a testament to its dedication to architectural excellence, the museum actively contributes to the preservation and documentation of architectural heritage in Finland. It partners with other institutions, architects, and scholars to preserve a vast archive that serves as a significant resource for those researching Finnish architectural history.

Havis Amanda Statue

Havis Amanda, widely referred to simply as "Manta," is a beloved statue. This renowned sculpture possesses great cultural and historical relevance, making it a must-see for travelers visiting the Finnish capital. Depicting a young lady emerging from the sea, Havis Amanda reflects the essence of Helsinki and its marine tradition, while also acting as a symbol of artistic expression and national identity.

Designed by renowned Finnish sculptor Ville Vallgren, Havis Amanda was erected in 1908 as part of a competition commissioned by the city. The statue's name is a mix of "Havis," referring to the city of Helsinki, and "Amanda," a popular name denoting feminine beauty and elegance. Vallgren's design was welcomed with both appreciation and controversy since its image of a nude woman emerging from the waves was considered provocative at the time.

The statue's location at the Market Square, a central and lively district of Helsinki, further enhances its significance. The Market Square has historically been a focus of trade, culture, and social interaction, making it a perfect spot for a symbol that symbolizes the city's spirit. Havis Amanda stands boldly in the midst of this busy plaza, becoming a focus point for both inhabitants and visitors.

Havis Amanda's creative worth rests not just in its aesthetics but also in its representation of the Art Nouveau style. The flowing lines, rich embellishments, and organic forms characteristic of Art Nouveau are all apparent in the statue's design. This artistic movement aspired to break away from established rules, embracing nature's impact and celebrating the confluence of art and life. Havis Amanda embodies this energy, symbolizing renewal, transformation, and the ever-changing aspect of the sea.

Beyond its visual appeal, Havis Amanda has a rich cultural and historical background. The statue was created during a time when Finland was struggling for national identity and autonomy, having only recently earned independence from Russia in 1917. Havis Amanda's rising from the sea might be considered as a metaphor for Finland's emergence as a sovereign nation, shaking off the chains of its history. This connection to the nation's history resonates powerfully with both locals and tourists, highlighting the statue's continuing relevance.

The monument also has a role in current Finnish traditions. Each year on April 30th, a tradition known as "Vappu" or May Day is observed across the country. Havis Amanda serves as the focal point of Helsinki's Vappu festivities. Students gather around the statue to place a white student cap, or "ylioppilaslakki," on her head, signifying the beginning of spring celebrations. This custom is a vivid exhibition of youthfulness, community, and the continuation of cultural history.

Havis Amanda's continued appeal is a tribute to its capacity to capture the imagination of both residents and tourists. Its symbolic significance, connection to Finnish history, and artistic charm make it a multidimensional attraction that speaks to many groups. Visitors can engage with the statue on various levels—appreciating its beauties, knowing its historical context, and engaging in modern customs.

Parliament House

As the seat of Finland's parliament, the building plays a crucial role in the country's democratic governance. Its design, history, and symbolism all contribute to a full understanding of this renowned structure.

Designed by architects Johan Sigfrid Sirén and Karl Johan Woldemar Lindroos, Parliament House was finished in 1931. The architects envisioned a neoclassical structure with a hint of functionalism, mixing heritage with modernity. The building's facade shows classical characteristics such as columns, pilasters, and a prominent pediment, which are typical of neoclassical architecture. However, the architects added a streamlined and simplified form, representative of the functionalist style, imbuing the structure with a feeling of contemporary aesthetics.

The location of Parliament House carries historical significance. It is placed at the border of Central Park and represents the boundary between the city center and the natural environs. This placement underlines the Finnish people's link to both urban life and the country's natural landscape. The park in front of the building serves as a venue for gatherings, demonstrations, and celebrations, allowing individuals to directly engage with the political process.

The interior of Parliament House is similarly intriguing. The main chamber, where parliamentary sessions are place, is noted by its semi-circular seating configuration. This design fosters openness and inclusivity, establishing a sense of equality among members of parliament. The ceiling has an outstanding fresco by artist Akseli Gallen-Kallela, titled "The Kalevala," representing episodes from the Finnish national epic. This artwork not only contributes to cultural relevance but also enhances the idea of national identity within the political realm.

Symbolism is intertwined throughout the building's architecture and ornamentation. The majestic flight of steps leading to the main entrance signifies the ascent towards democracy and enlightenment. The granite walls and columns convey strength and stability, symbolizing the resilience of Finnish democracy. Additionally, the building's external sculptures and reliefs pay homage to Finnish history and culture, with motifs reflecting topics such as work, education, and justice.

Parliament House also plays a key part in the political life of Finland. It houses the Parliament of Finland, which comprises 200 members that are elected by the voters. The building's architecture, with its circular chamber, invites collaboration and debate among delegates, symbolizing the values of participatory democracy. The accessibility of the facility allows individuals to observe debates and conversations, boosting transparency and civic involvement.

Over the years, Parliament House has undergone modifications and expansions to satisfy the increasing needs of the democratic process. The extension, constructed in 2004, provides contemporary facilities and meeting rooms for members of parliament and their employees.

Helsinki Olympic Stadium

Constructed for the 1940 Summer Olympics, which were ultimately postponed owing to World War II, the Helsinki Olympic Stadium boasts a historic background that spans decades. Its design, a remarkable blend of Functionalist and Modernist architectural styles, was the vision of architects Yrjö Lindegren and Toivo Jäntti. This innovative style melds simplicity with grandeur, creating an enduring structure that symbolizes Finland's architectural character.

The stadium's principal duty is to act as a host for a range of sporting events, including athletics, football (soccer), and even concerts. Its highlight is the perfectly kept track and field complex, surrounded by tiered seating that accommodates over 40,000 spectators. This amphitheater-style setup guarantees a spectacular perspective for every attendee, generating an exciting environment throughout events.

Beyond its sporting significance, the Helsinki Olympic Stadium retains tremendous cultural value. The Olympic Games, while never taking place in 1940, would have been a testament to international solidarity and athleticism. As such, the stadium's impact extends beyond sports, standing as a tribute to the tenacity and perseverance of a people who overcome the challenges brought by war.

Visitors to the stadium have the option to explore its inner passageways, where a painstakingly organized collection of memorabilia, photographs, and exhibitions tell the tale of Finland's sporting adventure. This immersive experience provides insight into the nation's sporting successes, historical landmarks, and the evolving significance of the stadium in molding the country's identity.

In 2020, the Helsinki Olympic Stadium underwent an intensive remodeling project to upgrade its facilities and ensure its future importance in the 21st century. This attempt aims to connect the stadium's historic legacy with modern conveniences, offering athletes and fans alike a seamless and enjoyable experience. The refurbished stadium offers increased accessibility, upgraded seats, and advanced technology for broadcasting and fan involvement.

The tower of the Helsinki Olympic Stadium is another striking element that attracts the mind of tourists. Rising to a height of nearly 70 meters, the tower affords panoramic views of the surrounding cityscape. It's a monument to the stadium's ongoing attractiveness that it remains one of the most popular attractions in Helsinki, offering an unequaled vantage point to enjoy the city's cityscape and urban layout.

The stadium continues to play a major role in the city's cultural and sporting landscape. Regularly hosting a diversity of events, from big international sporting contests to rock concerts, the Helsinki Olympic Stadium is a dynamic site that bridges the gap between entertainment and tradition. Its impact on Finnish society is apparent, generating a sense of national pride and fraternity.

Kamppi Chapel of Silence

The Kamppi Chapel of Silence is a wonderful architectural gem that offers both locals and tourists a tranquil sanctuary from urban turmoil. Designed by K2S Architects, this remarkable edifice has attracted global attention for its simple design, tranquil environment, and novel approach to contemporary spirituality.

Completed in 2012, the Kamppi Chapel of Silence serves as a testimony to modern architectural inventiveness. Its unusual oval shape is coated with a coating of spruce wood, which not only inspires a sensation of warmth but also easily fits with the surrounding surroundings. The exterior's curved wooden slats form an elaborate lattice that allows light to seep through, forming fascinating patterns on the chapel's interior surfaces.

Upon entering the chapel, guests are immersed in a serene ambiance, instantly escaping the rush and bustle of the metropolis outside. The interior space is highlighted by its curving walls, constructed from Finnish alder wood, which produces a warm cocoon-like environment. The delicate illumination pouring through the wooden exterior generates a play of light and shadow that is nothing short of captivating. With its calm design, the chapel offers a spot for contemplation, meditation, or simply finding solace in a moment of stillness.

One of the most notable elements of the Kamppi Chapel is its extraordinary acoustics. The hardwood walls and ceiling are designed to absorb sound, creating an ambiance where even the softest whisper becomes exaggerated. This novel acoustic design emphasizes introspection and solitude, allowing guests to indulge in inner meditation without the interruption of external sounds.

In a society driven by digital distractions and continual connectivity, the Kamppi Chapel of Silence serves as a haven for disconnecting and recentering. Visitors from all walks of life, regardless of their faith or background, are welcome to enter inside and take a pause from their daily activities. This inclusive mindset reflects the Finnish tradition of respecting personal space and privacy, generating an environment of openness and acceptance.

The chapel also serves as an exemplary example of sustainable building. The building's design integrates eco-friendly materials and energy-efficient solutions, aligning with Finland's dedication to environmental conscience. This sustainability not only testifies to the country's attention to responsible architecture but also adds to the overall sense of harmony that the church exudes.

The Kamppi Chapel is situated in Narinkka Square, a busy urban square recognized for its shopping and entertainment attractions. This juxtaposition of peacefulness against the urban backdrop provides a thought-provoking contrast, reminding visitors of the significance of balance in their lives.

Museum of Natural History

Stairways of MNH

The museum's primary objective is to enlighten and educate visitors about the diversity of life on Earth and the intricate relationships that define our planet's ecosystems, covering a wide range of subjects, including geology, paleontology, botany, and zoology, the museum provides a comprehensive overview of the natural sciences. One of the most striking elements of the organization is its large collection of specimens, including fossils, minerals, plants, and animals from diverse corners of the globe.

Upon entering the museum, visitors are instantly struck by the grandeur of the building's architecture. The combination of traditional and modern design elements creates an ambiance that is both inviting and awe-inspiring. The exhibits are painstakingly designed to educate visitors about the history of life on Earth, from the first bacteria to the complex ecosystems that exist today.

One of the museum's highlights is the paleontology department, which shows an astounding assortment of fossils. These relics from the distant past provide a look into the evolution of life forms and the changing landscapes of our planet. From towering dinosaur skeletons to exquisitely preserved ancient insects, this portion of the museum grabs the imagination of visitors and highlights the mysteries of prehistoric existence.

The participatory aspect of many exhibitions makes the Museum of Natural History distinct. Visitors have the option to participate in the displays through touch screens, multimedia presentations, and hands-on activities. This technique creates a deeper knowledge of scientific concepts and encourages a sense of curiosity and investigation. For younger visitors, the museum offers dedicated spaces that are both informative and amusing, making it a perfect location for families.

The Museum of Scientific History frequently hosts temporary exhibitions that dive into certain areas within the scientific sciences. These revolving exhibits ensure that there is always something fresh and intriguing to explore, even for repeat visitors. From in-depth explorations of biodiversity to analyses of climate change's influence on ecosystems, these shows keep the museum's offerings current and relevant.

The museum's mission to teaching extends beyond its exhibitions. It offers a range of instructional programs geared for different age groups, from students to adults. These activities include guided tours, workshops, and lectures by specialists in various subjects. For travelers seeking a deeper understanding of Finland's natural heritage, these courses provide a rare opportunity to engage with the scientific community and receive insights into ongoing research.

Suomen Kansallisooppera (Finnish National Opera)

Suomen Kansallisooppera, popularly known as the Finnish National Opera, is a world-class institution and is a cornerstone of Finland's thriving cultural scene, displaying a rich tapestry of opera, ballet, and other performing arts.

Founded in 1911, the Finnish National Opera has a rich history that follows Finland's quest to become an independent nation. The opera theater has served as a place for cultural expression, national pride, and creative creativity. Its foundation corresponded with the time when Finland was expressing its identity and strengthening its cultural foundations. Over the decades, the opera has continued to flourish, becoming a symbol of Finnish inventiveness and endurance.

The opera house's architecture is a beautiful blend of tradition and contemporary. The exterior displays a neoclassical façade, an homage to ageless architectural design. The inside, however, shocks guests with its contemporary aesthetics, delivering a perfect combination of sleek lines, warm wood tones, and vast spaces. The main auditorium is a masterpiece of acoustics and engineering, guaranteeing that every note, every word, reverberates with flawless clarity. The opera's design isn't only about functionality; it's an artistic statement in its own right.

What truly sets the Finnish National Opera apart is its devotion to musical excellence. The opera's repertory encompasses classical masterpieces and modern works, displaying a varied selection of productions that cater to different preferences. From the heart-wrenching arias of

Puccini to the vibrant choreography of modern dance, the opera delivers a sensory feast for audiences. Renowned foreign performers interact with local talents, increasing the cultural exchange that defines the opera's schedule.

For tourists, seeing a performance at the Finnish National Opera is a transformational experience. The grandeur of the theatre, the anticipation before the curtain rises, and the communal stillness when the music begins to create a sense of shared astonishment. Whether you're a seasoned opera aficionado or a first-time attendee, the emotional power of the performances is evident. The blend of music, storytelling, and visual extravaganza crosses language borders, making it accessible to audiences from around the world.

Beyond its main stage acts, the Finnish National Opera offers a number of programs to engage guests. Behind-the-scenes tours provide insights into the intricate workings of the opera, from costume design and set construction to rehearsals and technical aspects. Educational programs introduce young audiences to the magic of opera and ballet, nurturing an enthusiasm for the performing arts from an early age. Additionally, the opera house hosts special events, workshops, and debates that dive into the artistic process and the broader cultural scene.

Kallio District

Kallio Church

Originally an industrial working-class neighborhood, Kallio has transformed over the years into a hub of innovation, artistry, and urban growth. The district's history is still visible in its architecture, with a combination of well-preserved Art Nouveau buildings and mid-century constructions that reflect the tale of its progress. Walking around the streets, tourists can observe the shift from its industrial history to the contemporary present, capturing the spirit of Kallio's journey.

One of the distinctive qualities of Kallio is its vibrant atmosphere, built by a diverse and close-knit population. The region is noted for its friendly and welcoming climate, promoting a strong sense of belonging among both locals and visitors. This is best experienced through the various cafes, pubs, and street markets that populate the region, allowing abundant opportunities to engage with inhabitants and absorb the local culture. For a true sense of Finnish living, striking up talks with Kallio's pleasant locals is highly advised.

Art and creativity flourish in Kallio, visible through its numerous galleries, stores, and street art. The district has become a sanctuary for artists and designers, resulting in a dynamic arts culture that is continually growing. Visitors can visit distinctive galleries presenting contemporary art, witness live music events, or stumble upon vivid murals that adorn building facades, all of which add to the creative fabric that defines Kallio.

No exploration of Kallio is complete without indulging in its culinary offers. The district's cuisine culture is a fusion of traditional Finnish flavors and international influences, making it a haven for food connoisseurs. From quiet cafes selling freshly baked pastries to contemporary eateries providing inventive meals, Kallio caters to a range of tastes and preferences. This diversity reflects the cosmopolitan aspect of the district and parallels Helsinki's own cultural melting pot.

Kallio's charms extend beyond its metropolitan landscape. The region boasts various parks and recreational places, providing a breath of fresh air and tranquillity despite the city's bustle. For instance, Linnanmäki Amusement Park offers thrilling thrills and entertainment for families, while Tokoinranta Park offers a tranquil waterfront hideaway great for picnics or leisurely strolls. These spaces not only enhance the quality of life for inhabitants but also offer tourists a chance to unwind and enjoy nature.

Transportation in Kallio is convenient, enabling simple access to the rest of Helsinki. Trams and buses connect the district to other parts of the city, giving it a good starting place for exploring beyond its bounds. However, it's encouraged to explore Kallio by foot to fully immerse oneself in its character and find hidden jewels that may be missed when traveling by automobile.

Conclusion
Helsinki is a city that captivates with its architectural grandeur, cultural richness, and deep connection to nature. From historic landmarks to contemporary museums, from lively markets to tranquil green spaces, the Finnish capital offers a multidimensional experience that caters to a diverse spectrum of interests. With its beautiful blend of tradition and modernity, Helsinki draws travelers to discover its delights and immerse themselves in the distinctive tapestry of Finnish culture. Whether you're an architecture aficionado, a history buff, a nature lover, or a gourmet explorer, Helsinki promises an immersive journey that will leave an unforgettable impact on your travel memories.

Top Cuisine to Try Out

Helsinki also offers a delicious culinary experience that represents the country's rich cultural heritage and inventive attitude. From traditional Finnish meals to modern renditions, the city's food culture is a blend of flavors that cater to all palates. For travelers wishing to indulge in local gastronomy, there are numerous must-try dishes that encapsulate the essence of Helsinki's gastronomic scene. Here are the dishes that tourists might eat in Helsinki:

Kalakukko

Kalakukko is a savory pie that developed in the Finnish area of Savonia. It consists of a robust stuffing of fish, often perch or vendace, combined with pork and bacon. This tasty mixture is sealed in a rye crust, creating a wonderful balance of textures and tastes. The meal is customarily roasted for several hours in a wood-fired oven, enabling the flavors to mix and develop.

In Helsinki, you may find Kalakukko in many restaurants, cafes, and bakeries that specialize in traditional Finnish food. These establishments frequently take pleasure in using locally sourced ingredients, offering an authentic and fresh experience. Tourists looking to sample this meal might explore sites like market halls, such as the famed Hakaniemi Market Hall or the Old Market Hall (Vanha Kauppahalli), where they might locate vendors or cafés selling Kalakukko.

The experience of experiencing Kalakukko goes beyond only the taste. It's a cultural trip that connects you with Finland's history and traditions. As you cut into the crust and reveal the aromatic filling, you'll appreciate the expertise that goes into creating this meal. It's a reminder of the simple joys and strong bond with nature that the Finnish people enjoy.

While Kalakukko might be a deviation from normal tourist cuisine, it's a culinary journey that's worth venturing into. If you're not accustomed to Finnish flavors, be prepared for a substantial and rich blend of ingredients. The meal is commonly served with a side of lingonberry jam, which provides a tangy contrast to the savory richness of the pie.

Karjalanpiirakka

When exploring Helsinki's cuisine scene, encountering Karjalanpiirakka is a necessity. Originating from the region of Karelia, which runs between modern-day Finland and Russia, this pastry has become a vital element of Finnish cuisine. Its popularity has led to different variations and recipes, but the basic components remain consistent: the thin crust and the filling. The crust, commonly prepared from a blend of rye and wheat flour, is rolled out thinly to achieve a delicate balance between crispness and tenderness. The filling, generally consisting of rice porridge or mashed potatoes, is seasoned with salt and butter, offering a delicious and warming taste.

In Helsinki, you may enjoy Karjalanpiirakka in a variety of venues, from street food vendors to snug cafés. Many bakers take pride in producing these sweets using time-honored techniques passed down through generations. While enjoying Karjalanpiirakka, it's worth considering the cultural value it carries. It symbolizes Finnish strength and resourcefulness, as it was historically a way for Karelian women to produce a nourishing meal from simple items during tough times.

When ordering Karjalanpiirakka in Helsinki, consider complementing it with a dollop of butter and a sprinkling of egg butter or minced egg. This enriches the flavor profile and adds richness to each bite. Whether savored as a snack, light dinner, or part of a bigger Finnish feast, this pastry delivers an authentic sense of Finland's culinary heritage.

As a tourist, immersing oneself in the experience of experiencing Karjalanpiirakka is an opportunity to connect with Finnish culture on a deeper level. Beyond its wonderful taste, this dessert carries stories of tradition, resilience, and community.

Lohikeitto

Lohikeitto, or "salmon soup" in Finnish, is a famous comfort food that reflects the essence of Finland's relationship with the sea and forests. The soup normally comprises fresh salmon, potatoes, leeks, carrots, and sometimes dill, all mixed in a creamy broth. The ingredients mimic the seasonal product of the region, highlighting the relationship between the people and their environment. The inclusion of salmon, a staple in Finnish cuisine, hints at the country's reliance on its water bodies for nutrition.

The preparation of Lohikeitto is a delicate combination of flavors and textures. The salmon is gently simmered in the broth, enabling its natural taste to soak into the dish. The inclusion of fresh herbs like dill adds an aromatic dimension, enriching the whole experience. The soup's creamy base, frequently cooked with milk or cream, adds a comforting richness that complements the robust elements.

Enjoying Lohikeitto extends beyond its taste; it's an immersion into Finnish culture. In Helsinki, several restaurants and cafes serve this dish, giving guests a chance to partake in a genuine gastronomic experience. Whether in expensive eateries or intimate neighborhood spots, Lohikeitto brings people together around a shared enjoyment of food, generating a sense of community and warmth.

For tourists, Lohikeitto epitomizes the spirit of Finnish hospitality and the notion of "hygge," a warm and contented quality of life. It's a dish best served during the winter months, bringing comfort and peace in its creamy embrace. The soup's flavors inspire a sense of nostalgia, resonating with the history of Finland's nautical traditions and the significance of food as a unifying factor.

Hernekeitto

Hernekeitto, which translates to "pea soup" in English, is a simple yet flavorful dish that has been cherished by generations. The soup's core consists of green peas, often dry or frozen, which are cooked to perfection with a diversity of seasonings. These components commonly include ham, pork, or smoked meat, giving to the soup's powerful and delicious flavor. Some variations could replace meat with root vegetables, producing a vegetarian option that keeps the soup's nutritious essence.

What makes Hernekeitto particularly remarkable is its historical relevance. Dating back centuries, this dish has been a mainstay of Finnish cuisine, supplying sustenance during long, severe winters. Traditionally cooked in huge numbers, it was a cost-effective way to feed families and communities. Its ongoing popularity led to its establishment as a cultural symbol, spanning generations and becoming a treasured comfort dish.

In Helsinki, Hernekeitto is not simply a meal but an experience. It is popularly eaten in homes, restaurants, and cafes around the city. Many places take pride in giving their personal interpretation of the classic dish, typically integrating seasonal ingredients and new tweaks. Whether consumed as a single dish or paired with freshly baked rye bread, the flavors of Hernekeitto inspire a sense of warmth and comfort.

For tourists, tasting Hernekeitto is an opportunity to immerse themselves in Finnish culture. It provides an insight into the nation's history, tenacity, and culinary traditions. Many restaurants in Helsinki offer the soup as part of their menu, allowing guests the chance to enjoy an authentic flavor of Finland. In addition, locals take delight in sharing their culinary heritage, making it a fantastic way to participate in conversations and learn more about life in Helsinki.

Poronkäristys

The name "poronkäristys" stems from two Finnish words: "poro," which denotes reindeer, and "käristys," which refers to the manner of preparing the meat. To produce this meal, thin slices of reindeer meat are softly fried in a pan with butter or oil until they become crispy. This technique gives the meat a lovely texture and accentuates its rich flavors. The meal is frequently seasoned with salt and black pepper, and sometimes a bit of allspice for added warmth.

Poronkäristys maintains a special place in Finnish culture, representing the historical importance of reindeer herding to the indigenous Sámi people. Reindeer herding has been a key element of their way of life for millennia, providing nourishment and economic support. By savoring poronkäristys, travelers can connect with Finland's cultural heritage and pay homage to its indigenous traditions.

In Helsinki, tourists can find poronkäristys served at many restaurants and cafés, both traditional and contemporary. The dish is commonly served with sides such as mashed potatoes, lingonberry jam, and pickles, which complement the flavors and textures of the meat. The sharpness of lingonberry jam nicely balances the richness of the meat, providing a balanced blend of flavors.

For tourists seeking an authentic Finnish gastronomic experience, poronkäristys delivers a particular taste of the country's cuisine. It's a cuisine that not only exhibits the natural resources of Finland but also highlights the skillful technique of preparing and storing food, a practice strongly established in Finnish history.

Silakkapihvit

Silakkapihvit, often known as "fried Baltic herring patties," is a classic Finnish meal that delivers a wonderful and tasty taste of local cuisine. Found in Helsinki's restaurants and food booths, these savory pleasures give travelers a unique gourmet experience and a peek into Finland's culinary tradition.

Silakkapihvit starts with fresh Baltic herring, a staple of Finnish seas. The herring fillets are thoroughly deboned, assuring a bone-free and delightful dining experience. The fillets are then seasoned with a blend of traditional herbs and spices, which could include dill, parsley, and black pepper. This spice offers a pleasant blend of tastes that enhances the natural taste of the fish.

Next, the seasoned herring fillets are covered in a light batter, commonly made from a mixture of flour, eggs, and milk. This batter offers a crispy and golden surface to the patties when they are fried to perfection. The frying procedure results in a precise balance between the crispy outer layer and the tender, flaky herring inside, providing a textural contrast that is a hallmark of Silakkapihvit.

Silakkapihvit is commonly served with classic Finnish accompaniments that enrich the dish's overall experience. Boiled new potatoes, a dollop of lingonberry jam, and a sprig of fresh dill are frequent extras that enhance the flavors and make a well-rounded dinner. These aspects accentuate the traditional, locally sourced foods that are important to Finnish cuisine.

For travelers wanting a genuine gastronomic experience, trying Silakkapihvit is a must. Beyond the wonderful flavors, having this dish in Helsinki also delivers cultural information. It's a chance to engage with Finnish customs that have been passed down through centuries. While enjoying Silakkapihvit, guests can engage in talks with locals, discover stories behind the cuisine, and develop a deeper respect for the country's history and lifestyle.

Ruisleipä

Ruisleipä is a black, dense bread made mostly from whole rye flour, water, and a tiny amount of yeast or sourdough starter. Its peculiar flavor and texture are derived from the long fermenting process that can take up to 24 hours. The bread's gritty crumb and chewy firmness give it a substantial feel, making it a great match for both sweet and savory toppings.

In Helsinki, you'll find Ruisleipä in the heart of every local's daily diet. Its appeal originates from its nutritional benefits and its position in Finnish history. Ruisleipä has been a staple for ages, dating back to times when rye was one of the only crops that could survive in the tough Nordic climate. Its capacity to endure the harsh conditions of the region made it an important element in the Finnish diet, and this relevance remains to this day.

While modern culinary options have proliferated in Helsinki, Ruisleipä remains a valued component of Finnish identity. It's not uncommon to see people enjoying an open-faced sandwich topped with herring, salmon, or cold meats, all nestled on a slice of this nutritious bread. In recent years, there's also been a rebirth of interest in traditional and regionally derived cuisine, enhancing Ruisleipä's popularity even further.

For tourists visiting Helsinki, trying Ruisleipä is not just about savoring a culinary delight, but also about comprehending the cultural significance of the cuisine. Many bakeries and cafes offer freshly baked loaves, delivering an authentic experience. Some establishments even provide guided tours or workshops that showcase the bread-making process, allowing tourists to observe the skill behind this culinary legacy.

Salmiakki

Salmiakki, a peculiar Finnish delight, provides travelers with a unique taste experience in the center of Helsinki. Known for its divisive flavor, Salmiakki is a type of salty licorice that maintains a special position in Finnish culture and cuisine.

Derived from ammonium chloride, Salmiakki's distinctly salty and somewhat acidic taste has its roots in the Nordic tradition of blending salt and licorice. Finnish people have established a deep fondness for this treat through the years, making it a vital part of their cultural character. The flavor is an acquired taste, with reactions ranging from excitement to perplexity among people eating it for the first time.

Tourists seeking to enjoy Salmiakki in Helsinki have many possibilities. Local supermarkets and specialty candy shops, including the famous "Fazer" brand, provide a wide choice of Salmiakki goods, from moderate to extremely salty versions.

For a more authentic experience, visitors can explore traditional Finnish markets such as the Old Market Hall (Vanha Kauppahalli), where traders often offer Salmiakki available for sampling and purchase.

Beyond its peculiar taste, Salmiakki carries cultural value. Finnish people commonly utilize it as a sign of their distinct national identity, and it's even been put into items like ice cream and chocolate to appeal to both locals and tourists. For travelers looking to delve deeper into Finnish culture, trying Salmiakki becomes an experience in understanding the intricacies of local preferences and traditions.

When sampling Salmiakki, an open attitude is needed. While it might not be everyone's cup of tea, embracing the experience of eating a new and unfamiliar flavor is a terrific way to connect with the local culture. Many travelers find the experience of discussing their thoughts on Salmiakki with locals to be a fun conversation starter, opening the door to talks about Finnish customs and tastes.

Mustikkapiirakka

Mustikkapiirakka translates to "blueberry pie" in English, and it's a renowned delicacy that embodies simplicity, flavor, and tradition. Helsinki, the capital of Finland, provides visitors the option to experience this wonderful dessert in diverse settings, from cozy cafes to local bakeries.

At its center, Mustikkapiirakka includes a buttery and crumbly crust that encases a large covering of fresh blueberries. The blueberries are often locally procured, underscoring the importance of employing seasonal ingredients in Finnish cuisine. The filling is sweetened, letting the natural tanginess of the blueberries show through. It's easy to find modest changes in the recipe, with some versions adding a hint of vanilla or even a dab of whipped cream on top for added pleasure.

Tourists can enjoy Mustikkapiirakka in many ways during their visit to Helsinki. Many cafés and bakeries proudly serve this treat, allowing guests to taste it as a standalone dessert or as part of a pleasant coffee break. Whether it's savored with a cup of rich Finnish coffee or a soothing cup of tea, the mix of flavors delivers a comfortable and authentic sense of Finnish culture.

Beyond its exquisite taste, Mustikkapiirakka carries cultural value. It's a dish that binds generations, commonly prepared in Finnish households during the summer months when blueberries are in season. This culinary heritage symbolizes the intimate connection that Finns have with their natural environment and the importance of embracing local resources.

For tourists wishing to learn more about Finnish cuisine and culture, experiencing Mustikkapiirakka is a must. It's a gateway to understanding the nation's appreciation for simplicity, nature, and the pleasures of sharing wonderful cuisine with loved ones. The experience of having this dessert in Helsinki provides an insight into the heart of Finnish living and offers a delectable memory that will stay with tourists long after they've gone home.

Korvapuusti

Also known as cinnamon rolls, these exquisite pastries are strongly established in Finnish culture and offer a tasty look into the local culinary scene.

Korvapuusti are characterized by their smooth, somewhat sweet dough infused with scented cinnamon and a dash of cardamom. The dough is precisely rolled out and generously slathered with a mixture of butter, sugar, and cinnamon before being firmly coiled up and cut into separate parts. The outcome is a spiral of delight that's baked till golden brown, filling the air with an intoxicating smell.

The word "korvapuusti" translates to "slap on the ear" in English, which is claimed to refer to the traditional shape of the pastry resembling an ear. Whether or not this is the genuine origin of the name, it lends a whimsical element to the pastry's attraction.

Locals and visitors alike commonly enjoy korvapuusti as a treat with a cup of coffee, making it a great complement to a quiet break. In Helsinki, these pastries can be obtained in a range of settings, from traditional bakeries to trendy cafes. Some places even put their own unique twist on the basic dish, producing variations with fillings like apple, blueberry, or even chocolate.

One of the greatest places to experience the original charm of korvapuusti is at local markets such as the Old Market Hall (Vanha Kauppahalli). Here, you may not only relish the famous cinnamon rolls but also engage with the lively ambiance and mingle with the friendly vendors. Another alternative is to visit historic bakeries like Fazer, a renowned Finnish brand that has been delighting taste buds for decades.

For tourists seeking to dive deeper into Finnish culinary traditions, there are possibilities to learn the craft of producing korvapuusti through baking classes provided in Helsinki. These sessions not only provide hands-on experience but also offer insights into the history and cultural significance of the pastry.

Conclusion
Exploring Helsinki's culinary scene is a journey that introduces tourists to the heart and spirit of Finnish culture. From traditional cuisine anchored in history to modern adaptations that reflect the city's cosmopolitan milieu, Helsinki provides a broad assortment of flavors that represent the country's natural richness. Whether indulging in robust stews, tasting freshly caught fish, or enjoying the warmth of Finnish hospitality over coffee and pastries, travelers are likely to find

a gourmet excursion that leaves a lasting memory of their time in this enchanting Nordic capital.

Best Time To Visit

As a tourist, choosing the optimal time to visit Helsinki is vital to making the most of your experience. The optimum time to explore Helsinki mostly relies on your interests, weather preferences, and the type of activities you desire to partake in during your trip.

Summer, ranging from June through August, is traditionally considered the primary tourism season in Helsinki. The city actually comes alive during these months, bringing visitors a wealth of outdoor activities, festivals, and extended daylight hours. The renowned Midnight Sun phenomenon happens in June and July, with the sun just dropping beyond the horizon, providing you ample opportunity to explore the city even during the late hours. The moderate temperatures ranging from 15°C to 25°C (59°F to 77°F) make it excellent for outdoor activities such as sightseeing, picnics, and boat cruises to the surrounding islands. Suomenlinna, a UNESCO World Heritage Site located on an island, is a popular attraction accessible by a short boat journey, featuring historical landmarks and magnificent views.

However, it's vital to know that summer is also the prime tourist season, resulting in heavier crowds and higher hotel expenses. It's advisable to reserve accommodations well in advance if you want to come during this season.

Should you prefer milder temperatures and fewer crowds, consider visiting Helsinki during the shoulder seasons of spring (April to May) or fall (September to October). During spring, the city gradually awakens from its winter slumber, and the blossoming parks and gardens create a magnificent backdrop for your travels. Fall shows Helsinki's gorgeous foliage as the trees change color, creating a peaceful and serene ambiance. These seasons offer average temperatures ranging from 5°C to 15°C (41°F to 59°F) and are great for individuals who like a quieter ambiance while still being able to enjoy outdoor activities comfortably.

For those seeking a unique experience, winter from December to February might be a magical time to visit Helsinki. While temperatures can drop dramatically, ranging from -5°C to -15°C (23°F to 5°F), the city changes into a winter paradise. The classic Christmas markets, such as the one in Senate Square, offer lovely local goods and seasonal delights. Additionally, you have the option to experience the stunning Northern Lights if you journey a bit further north from the city.

To make the most of your winter vacation, embrace the Finnish notion of "hygge," which stresses coziness and warmth. Engage in traditional pastimes like drinking a hot cup of glögi (mulled wine) or unwinding in a sauna, a classic feature of Finnish culture.

Conclusion
The best time to visit Helsinki depends on your particular interests and the type of experience you seek. Summer brings exciting festivals and extended daylight, spring and fall provide milder weather and fewer crowds, and winter offers a unique opportunity to enjoy Finnish customs in a snow-covered backdrop. Regardless of the season, Helsinki's charm, cultural attractions, and magnificent scenery ensure a wonderful journey. It's advisable to plan your vacation in advance, considering elements like weather, activities, and

budget to ensure a memorable and enjoyable stay in this enchanting Nordic capital.

Traveling Itinerary

With a well-planned 1-week vacation schedule, you may explore most of what Helsinki has to offer. Let's go on a memorable tour through this picturesque Scandinavian jewel.

Day 1: Arrival and City Orientation
Arrive at Helsinki-Vantaa Airport and settle into your centrally located hotel. After checking in, enjoy a leisurely stroll to the landmark Senate Square, surrounded by neoclassical buildings, including the imposing Helsinki Cathedral. Enjoy the spectacular city views from the cathedral's steps and discover the historic core of Helsinki. In the evening, eat some Finnish food at a local restaurant and relax by the waterfront.

Day 2: Exploring Design Districts and Art Museums
Start your day with a substantial Finnish breakfast at the hotel. Then, immerse yourself in the city's design culture by exploring the Design District. Wander through unique boutiques, galleries, and workshops displaying Finnish design expertise. Afterward, visit the Design Museum to learn about the evolution of Finnish design. In the afternoon, explore the Ateneum Art Museum, famed for its magnificent collection of Finnish art spanning many centuries.

Day 3: Island Hopping and Seaside Charm
Catch a ferry to Suomenlinna, a UNESCO World Heritage-listed sea fortress sprawled across multiple interconnecting islands. Explore its ancient fortifications, museums, and lovely scenery. Enjoy a picnic lunch while staring over the Baltic Sea. Return to the city and spend the evening at the busy

Market Square, where you can indulge in local foods and browse for unique gifts.

Day 4: Contemporary Art and Sauna Culture
Visit the Kiasma Museum of Contemporary Art, noted for its avant-garde shows and thought-provoking installations. Experience a taste of true Finnish culture by indulging in the city's sauna tradition. Head to Löyly, a new public sauna facility by the sea, for a peaceful sauna session followed by a refreshing plunge in the Baltic seas.

Day 5: Day Trip to Porvoo
Take a day trip to Porvoo, a lovely medieval village located about an hour's drive from Helsinki. Wander through its cobbled lanes adorned with bright wooden cottages, art galleries, and stores. Visit the Porvoo Cathedral and enjoy a leisurely lunch at a nearby café. Return to Helsinki in the evening.

Day 6: Natural Beauty and National Museum
Explore the magnificent vegetation of Nuuksio National Park, located just outside the city. Hike through calm woodlands, observe tranquil lakes, and bond with nature. In the afternoon, visit the National Museum of Finland to learn about the country's history, culture, and folklore.

Day 7: Seurasaari Open-Air Museum and Farewell Dinner
Visit the Seurasaari Open-Air Museum, an enchanting place that highlights traditional Finnish architecture and culture. Walk around the tranquil parks filled with old buildings and learn about the country's agricultural heritage. In the evening, enjoy a farewell meal at a fine dining restaurant, relishing excellent Finnish delicacies and reflecting on the fantastic experiences of your week in Helsinki.

Conclusion

A 1-week trip to Helsinki guarantees a well-rounded tour of this interesting city. From its dynamic design culture to its ancient buildings, from its modern art scene to its natural beauty, Helsinki provides a broad selection of experiences that cater to all kinds of people. By following this carefully prepared schedule, you'll be able to make the most of your time in Helsinki, generating lasting memories and developing a closer connection with Finland's capital.

Visiting On a Budget

Helsinki, the dynamic capital of Finland, offers an enticing blend of modern design, rich history, and gorgeous natural surroundings, making it a great destination for budget-conscious travelers. With a little planning and insider knowledge, you can experience the finest of Helsinki without breaking the bank.

Accommodation
To start your budget-friendly travel, try staying in hostels or budget hotels located near the city center. These options provide handy access to public transportation, activities, and restaurants while keeping your accommodation prices in check. Additionally, you might consider Airbnb rentals or guesthouses for affordable alternatives.

Transportation
Helsinki's well-connected public transit system, comprising trams, buses, and the metro, provides a cheap method to move around. Purchase a Helsinki Card, which offers unlimited trips on public transit along with free or subsidized access to several museums and attractions. Walking and cycling are also wonderful ways to explore the little city while enjoying its lovely streets and waterfront.

Free and Low-Cost Attractions
Helsinki provides a wealth of free and low-cost attractions that allow you to immerse yourself in the city's culture and history. Wander through the famed Esplanade Park, a gorgeous green spot regularly hosting free concerts and events. Discover the magnificent architecture of Senate Square, dominated by the historic Helsinki Cathedral. The neighboring

Market Square is an excellent area to sample local street food and enjoy the river vista.

Museums and Galleries
Many of Helsinki's museums provide free admission on certain days or during specific hours. The Kiasma Museum of Contemporary Art, for instance, gives free admittance on the first Friday of every month. The National Museum of Finland provides a glimpse into the nation's history and culture at a reasonable price. Remember to check each museum's website for latest information on their fees and timetables.

Outdoor Escapes
Nature enthusiasts will appreciate Helsinki's many natural spaces and accessible outdoor activities. Experience the allure of Nuuksio National Park, located a short train trip away, where hiking trails snake through beautiful forests, lakes, and rocky landscapes. Seurasaari Open-Air Museum can be enjoyed for a small cost.

Affordable Eats
Dining out doesn't have to deplete your pocketbook in Helsinki. Opt for local cafés, bistros, and food vendors for budget-friendly lunches. Savor a taste of Finnish cuisine with delicacies like karjalanpiirakka (savory pastries) or salmon soup. The Hietalahti Market Hall offers a broad choice of food stalls, allowing you to try numerous delicacies without overspending.

Local Markets
Exploring local markets is not only a frugal way to discover Helsinki but also an opportunity to mingle with the people. In addition to the aforementioned Market Square, the Hakaniemi Market Hall offers fresh fruit, baked products, and inexpensive

souvenirs. Remember to haggle pricing when purchasing things from the market merchants.

Seasonal Savings
Timing your vacation to Helsinki can considerably effect your costs. Summer is the prime tourist season, with better weather and longer days, but it also comes with higher hotel and activity fees. Consider visiting during the shoulder seasons of spring and fall when rates tend to be more budget-friendly, and you may still enjoy great weather.

Conclusion
Helsinki provides a wealth of economical options for those seeking an enriching experience without overspending. By planning your hotel, transportation, attractions, and dining properly, you can see the city's diverse culture, breathtaking landscapes, and architectural wonders while keeping within your budget. Whether you're meandering through parks, appreciating ancient landmarks, or relishing local cuisine, Helsinki on a budget is an adventure waiting to be found.

Getting Around

Helsinki also boasts a seamless and efficient transportation network that makes moving about the city a breeze for tourists. With a combination of public transportation choices, well-maintained highways, and pedestrian-friendly streets, touring Helsinki is a lovely experience.

Public Transportation
Helsinki features an efficient public transit system that includes buses, trams, and the metro. The well-connected network ensures that travelers may easily reach all main attractions. The trams are a popular choice, providing a lovely way to experience the city while getting about efficiently. The metro, on the other hand, offers a speedy route to go across the city, making it particularly helpful for greater distances.

Helsinki Card
For travellers searching for a hassle-free way to get around, the Helsinki Card is a terrific solution. This all-inclusive pass enables unlimited travels on public transit, including buses, trams, and the metro. It also grants free entrance to various museums and attractions, making it a cost-effective solution for those wishing to explore multiple places.

Biking
Helsinki is a bike-friendly city with well-marked bike lanes and dedicated riding routes. Many streets have designated lanes, and numerous bike rental services are accessible for tourists. Biking is not only an eco-friendly alternative but also a wonderful way to explore the city at a leisurely pace, giving you the chance to find hidden jewels and absorb in the local vibe.

Walking
Helsinki's tiny city core is great for pedestrians. Most important sights are within walking distance of each other, making it convenient to explore on foot. The city's design contains well-maintained walkways, pedestrian crossings, and pedestrian-only zones, assuring a safe and comfortable walking experience.

Ferries
Helsinki's unique topography, bordered by the Baltic Sea and several islands, allows options to use ferries for transit. The Suomenlinna boat, for instance, carries travelers to the UNESCO-listed Suomenlinna sea fortification, a famous tourist site. Additionally, ferries connect the city to adjacent islands, allowing travelers to appreciate the archipelago's splendor.

Taxi and Ride-Sharing
Taxis are commonly available in Helsinki and provide a convenient way to move around, especially during the evenings or when carrying large luggage. Ride-sharing services like Uber are also active, offering an alternative to regular taxis.

Car Rentals
While public transportation is good, some tourists might prefer the freedom of hiring a car. Helsinki's road system is well-maintained, and driving in the city is generally uncomplicated. However, keep in mind that parking in the city center might be restricted and expensive, so it's wise to investigate parking possibilities in advance.

Navigating the City
Helsinki is noted for its efficient signage and excellent wayfinding, making it easy for tourists to traverse. Street signs, maps, and directions are frequently provided in both Finnish and English, enabling visitors make their way around without problem.

City Planning
Helsinki's smart urban design and commitment to sustainability are visible in its transportation alternatives. The city supports the use of eco-friendly modes of transportation to reduce carbon emissions and promote a healthy lifestyle. This devotion is shown in the availability of bike lanes, well-connected public transportation, and attempts to decrease traffic congestion.

Conclusion
Helsinki provides travelers a selection of efficient and convenient transit options for experiencing the city. From an extensive public transportation network to biking, walking, and even boats, travelers may easily access the city's myriad attractions. Whether you're interested in experiencing the local culture or admiring the gorgeous architecture, Helsinki's transit system guarantees that you can explore the city with ease and make the most of your visit.

Shopping for Souvenirs

When it comes to enjoying the rich culture and unique vibe of a city, there's no better way to encapsulate the memories of your journey than by indulging in some souvenir shopping. Helsinki souvenirs are a representation of this city's many qualities, making the shopping experience a vital element of any tourist's stay.

As you wander Helsinki's bustling streets, you'll find that souvenir shops are strewn throughout the city, notably in popular districts like the Market Square, Esplanadi, and the Design District. These businesses offer a wide assortment of things that express the character of Helsinki, from traditional Finnish craftsmanship to contemporary design pieces.

Traditional Finnish Crafts and Artifacts
One of the most sought-after types of souvenirs in Helsinki is traditional Finnish workmanship. Items like Kalevala jewelry, which draws inspiration from Finnish mythology, and Sámi handicrafts are popular selections. Visitors can also find intricately carved wooden goods, such as Kuksa cups and cutlery, showing the mastery of Finnish woodworkers. The distinctive Moomin characters, designed by Tove Jansson, are also a favorite with travelers, with an abundance of Moomin-themed items available, including books, toys, and home goods.

Contemporary Finnish Design
Helsinki's position as a design capital is well-deserved, and this is reflected in the large choice of contemporary design objects available for purchase. Brands like Marimekko and Iittala are renowned for Finnish design and offer products that

integrate aesthetics with practicality. Marimekko is recognized for its colorful and bold prints, which can be found on apparel, luggage, and home textiles. Iittala, on the other hand, concentrates on minimalist glassware and dinnerware, showcasing the everlasting elegance of Finnish design.

Culinary Delights
No visit to Helsinki would be complete without indulging in its culinary scene, and taking home some Finnish food items can be a pleasant memento option. The legendary Fazer chocolates, famed for their high-quality taste, are a delicious treat appreciated by locals and visitors alike. Reindeer jerky and cloudberries in jams or liqueurs are also unusual options that encapsulate the essence of Finnish cuisine.

Exploring Souvenir Shopping Hotspots
The Market Square, or Kauppatori, is a busy hub in the center of Helsinki that offers a large assortment of souvenirs. From fresh vegetables and traditional food items to handicrafts and clothing, this market is a treasure mine for travelers seeking real Finnish products. The market's proximity to the waterfront also makes it an attractive site to browse while enjoying views of the Baltic Sea.

Esplanadi, widely referred to as the "Boulevard of Helsinki," is another destination for souvenir purchasing. This tree-lined road is home to a range of retailers, ranging from high-end boutiques to local design stores. It's an excellent destination to find Finnish fashion, jewelry, and home decor products that represent the city's sense of flair.

For individuals interested in contemporary design, the Design District is a must-visit location. This district is teeming with design shops, studios, and galleries, offering a curated variety of Finnish and Nordic design goods. From furniture and lighting to clothes and accessories, the Design District provides a unique shopping experience for design fans.

Cultural Etiquette and Tips
While shopping for souvenirs in Helsinki, it's vital to keep in mind some cultural etiquette and suggestions. Finnish people admire honesty, simplicity, and quality. Engaging in respectful and clear interactions with shops is welcomed. Bargaining is not a typical habit in Finnish shops, thus it's advisable to accept the prices as posted.

Conclusion
In the midst of Helsinki's lively streets and attractive districts, the experience of souvenir buying comes alive. The broad choice of traditional crafts, contemporary design elements, and culinary delights means that every traveler may discover a piece of Helsinki to take home. The city's link to its history, culture, and design ethos is brilliantly portrayed in the souvenirs on offer, making each item a tangible remembrance of an extraordinary journey. Whether wandering through the Market Square, discovering the Design District, or meandering down Esplanadi, souvenir shopping in Helsinki is an enriching experience that encompasses the city's essence and personality.

Tour Package Options

When organizing a vacation to Helsinki, you'll find a broad choice of tour package options that cater to various interests and preferences. From exploring the city's rich history and architecture to enjoying its vibrant culture and natural beauty, there's something for every sort of traveler.

Cultural Delights Package
Immerse yourself in Helsinki's cultural scene with this package. Visit prominent landmarks such as the UNESCO-listed Suomenlinna Sea Fortress, which offers a look into the city's history. Explore the Helsinki Cathedral and the Temppeliaukio Church, known as the Rock Church, both architectural marvels. The package might also include guided excursions to places like the Ateneum Art Museum and the Kiasma Museum of Contemporary Art, where you can appreciate Finnish inventiveness.

Design and Architecture Package
Helsinki is a hotspot for design enthusiasts. This bundle focuses on the city's creative architecture and design culture. You'll see gems like the Design Museum, highlighting Finland's design evolution. The Kamppi Chapel, sometimes referred to as the "Chapel of Silence," is another landmark, showing a simple style. The tour can also take you to Design District Helsinki, a dynamic district full of boutiques, galleries, and studios.

Natural Wonders & Scenic Beauty Package
For nature lovers, this package displays the gorgeous landscapes surrounding Helsinki. Explore Nuuksio National Park, just a short drive away, and luxuriate in its beautiful

forests, quiet lakes, and hiking routes. A boat journey to the adjacent archipelago is another choice, where you may appreciate the serene beauty of the Baltic Sea and its islands.

Sauna and Wellness Package
Sauna culture is firmly established in Finnish tradition. This package allows you to enjoy the authentic Finnish sauna routine. Enjoy visits to public saunas like Löyly, where you can combine the sauna experience with a refreshing swim in the Baltic Sea. The package could also include spa treatments, delivering a complete wellness holiday.

Culinary Exploration Package
Delve into Finnish cuisine with this package, savoring classic delicacies including Karelian pastries, reindeer, and salmon. Experience local marketplaces like the Old Market Hall and Hakaniemi Market, where you can sample fresh food and handcrafted delicacies. You might also take part in a culinary lesson to uncover the secrets of Finnish delicacies.

Urban Adventure Package
For an urban trip, opt for this package that introduces you to Helsinki's dynamic city life. Explore the busy Market Square, Senate Square, and the colorful streets of the Kallio area. Bike tours or Segway rides could be included to navigate the city's sights conveniently.

Seasonal Special Package
Helsinki's appeal fluctuates with the seasons. In summer, experience the Midnight Sun and outdoor festivals. In winter, view the magnificent Northern Lights and visit the Christmas markets. This bundle changes to the time of year, ensuring you get the most out of each season.

Family-Friendly Package
If you're traveling with family, this package caters to both adults and children. Explore family-oriented attractions like the Helsinki Zoo, the Linnanmäki Amusement Park, and the Sea Life Helsinki Aquarium. The program could also include interactive tours and activities suitable for all ages.

Conclusion
Helsinki provides a multitude of tour package options, each appealing to different interests and preferences. Whether you're a history buff, a wildlife enthusiast, a design lover, or a foodie, there's a package that meets your taste. Consider the cultural, architectural, natural, wellness, culinary, and seasonal aspects of the city to find the best tour package for your Helsinki vacation.

Tourist Safety Tips

Ensuring the safety of tourists is crucial for every travel destination, and Helsinki is no different. Helsinki offers a safe environment for travelers. To fully enjoy your vacation in Helsinki, it's vital to be aware of numerous safety recommendations that can enhance your experience and minimize potential risks.

Personal Belongings
Just as in any other city, it's advisable to keep a tight eye on your personal belongings, such as wallets, phones, and cameras. Pickpocketing can occur in busy settings, so utilize anti-theft bags or pouches and avoid exhibiting expensive items openly.

Emergency Numbers
Familiarize yourself with Finland's emergency numbers. The worldwide number for police, fire, and medical assistance is 112. It's always smart to have this number saved on your phone and know how to ask for help in English.

Accommodation Safety
Choose accommodations in safe neighborhoods. Most areas in Helsinki are safe, however, it's still a good idea to investigate and read reviews about the region before reserving your accommodation. Make sure your accommodation has sufficient security measures in place.

Public Transportation
Helsinki boasts an effective public transit system, comprising buses, trams, and the metro. While taking public

transportation, be mindful of your things, especially during rush hours.

Natural Environment
Helsinki's gorgeous natural settings are a big magnet for travelers. If you plan on trekking or exploring parks, use established routes and obey the local guidelines. Be prepared for shifting weather conditions and carry suitable gear.

Local Laws and Customs
Familiarize oneself with local laws and customs to avoid inadvertent crimes. Finland has severe laws on drinking and driving, and jaywalking is forbidden. Respect the local culture and manners, such as removing shoes while entering someone's home.

Health and Travel Insurance
It's advisable to get comprehensive health and travel insurance to cover any unforeseen medical expenditures or travel delays. The European Health Insurance Card (EHIC) can also be useful for EU nationals.

Scams & Tourist Traps
While Helsinki is reasonably safe from scammers, it's still important to keep watchful. Avoid dealing with persons who seem unduly persistent or proposing deals that sound too good to be true. Stick to reliable tour providers and establishments.

Street Safety
Helsinki's streets are generally safe to walk, even at night. However, it's advisable to keep to well-lit regions and key roadways. If you plan to tour the city after dark, consider traveling in a group.

Extreme Weather Precautions
Finland endures harsh weather conditions, especially in winter. Dress in layers, use appropriate footwear and cover exposed skin to prevent frostbite. Follow weather forecasts and advisories.

Food and Water Safety
Helsinki's food and water are generally safe to ingest. However, if you have any dietary limitations or concerns, mention them clearly when dining out. Bottled water is easily available if you prefer it over tap water.

By following these safety guidelines, you can have a delightful and worry-free experience while touring Helsinki. Remember that while safety measures are necessary, they shouldn't discourage you from enjoying the city's rich culture, history, and attractions.

Festival and Events

Throughout the year, Helsinki offers a number of festivals and events that exhibit its unique traditions, arts, and entertainment. From music and dance to food and design, Helsinki provides a varied choice of activities for travelers to immerse themselves in.

One of the most anticipated events in Helsinki is the Vappu festival, celebrated on the 1st of May. Also known as May Day, this celebration honors the entrance of spring and the end of winter. Locals and visitors assemble in great numbers to enjoy picnics, wear white student caps, and revel in various forms of entertainment. The celebratory environment, complete with bright balloons and cheery music, makes Vappu a remarkable experience.

For music fans, the Tuska Open Air Metal Festival in late June is a must-attend event. It's one of Europe's top metal events, drawing fans from around the world to see spectacular performances by both foreign and local metal acts. The three-day festival takes place in the heart of Helsinki, delivering a headbanging experience amidst an energetic crowd.

July comes the Helsinki International Film Festival, popularly known as Love & Anarchy. This event honors the art of cinema by playing a broad selection of international films. Movie fans can enjoy a mix of contemporary masterpieces, independent movies, and thought-provoking documentaries. The festival gives a platform for budding filmmakers and offers a chance for attendees to join in conversations and seminars.

For anyone interested in design and aesthetics, Helsinki Design Week in September is a must-visit. This event promotes Finnish and international design in numerous aspects, including fashion, furniture, and architecture. The city becomes a center of creative exhibitions, workshops, and talks, attracting both professionals and design aficionados.

Foodies should mark their calendars for the Taste of Helsinki festival, traditionally held in June. This gastronomic festival comprises some of the city's greatest restaurants and chefs, allowing a chance to sample wonderful meals crafted from the freshest local ingredients. It's a fantastic opportunity to explore Finnish cuisine and indulge in culinary pleasures.

In December, the festive season comes alive with the Helsinki Christmas Market. Set against the backdrop of the city's historic Senate Square, the market creates a magnificent ambiance with festive decorations, handicrafts, and traditional Finnish delights. Visitors can browse for unique items, taste warm mulled wine, and immerse themselves in the atmosphere of Christmas.

Art aficionados will appreciate the Night of the Arts, hosted annually in August. This festival transforms the streets, galleries, and museums of Helsinki into an open-air cultural playground. Performances, exhibitions, and interactive installations bring art to life, enabling both locals and tourists to participate in varied artistic forms.

Conclusion
Helsinki's festivals and events offer a complete overview of the city's culture, arts, and customs. From music and cinema to design and gastronomic delights, there's something for

everyone to enjoy throughout the year. These meetings not only provide entertainment but also generate possibilities for cultural interchange and absorption into the heart of Finnish society. Whether you're a metalhead, a cinephile, a design enthusiast, or simply someone trying to experience the local way of life, Helsinki's festivals will leave you with memorable memories and a better understanding of this dynamic city.